Return To

**OUTDOOR EDUCATION**
6401 Linda Vista Rd
San Diego, Ca 92111
att: William VanArsdale

Classroom Out-of-Doors

# Classroom Out-of-Doors

## EDUCATION THROUGH SCHOOL CAMPING

by
Wilbur Schramm
Director, Institute for Communication Research
Stanford University

for the

W.K. Kellogg Foundation
BATTLE CREEK, MICHIGAN

SEQUOIA PRESS/PUBLISHERS
KALAMAZOO, MICHIGAN

# FOREWORD

FROM ITS BEGINNING, the W. K. Kellogg Foundation has had particular concern for the young, this being especially set forth in its original Articles of Association which defined the guiding purpose as ". . . dedicated to improving the health, education, and well-being of children and youth." In the early 1930s, the organization's founder departed from his usual laissez-faire policy with regard to the Foundation to make a philanthropic suggestion to the Board of Trustees by asking: "Aren't we going to have a camping program for children?"

A resultant camping program was in connection with Battle Creek's Ann J. Kellogg School and its remedial services for handicapped children. The camp on Pine Lake became essentially a summer extension of the special education carried on in the city during the winter months and practicality soon indicated that such camp become a year-round one—a pattern thus being set for the several camps subsequently established and operated by the Foundation.

One of the latter camps became the location for the still-thriving outdoor education program of the Battle Creek Public Schools. At about the same time, the Foundation joined with the Michigan Conservation Department to promote a statewide school camping effort. In time, the idea of school camping spread to educational systems in the East, in Texas, in California, and to many locations over the nation. Since then, observations of the varied programs and of results from Foundation grants to the American Camping Association and of studies of the *Time-Life* camps in the East have helped to keep alive and strengthen the belief of many educators that outdoor education has special values which should become integral parts of public school systems of the country.

In 1946, a veteran of the Foundation's own camping staff went to Southern California to aid in the launching of a San Diego City-County Camping Program and, over the succeeding years, more than 250,000 boys and girls of the San Diego area have benefitted from educational experiences in a system of camps within mountains some thirty miles from the metropolitan area.

During the subsequent two decades, the policies, programs, and achievements have made San Diego's outdoor education one of the finest anywhere. Conservation learning—not just recreation, important as the latter is—has been emphasized. The camps have also been "schools for citizenship" where sixth-grade children come to grips with the realities of living, playing, and working together, and where there is admirable integration of youngsters of Caucasian, Negro, Oriental, and Spanish-American ancestry. And there truly has been overall support of this school camping program now grown to serve some 17,000 students annually. A locally structured camping commission, collaborating school districts throughout the county, and parents participating through the payment of camp fees: these are evidences that the entire program is a community venture. Perhaps the most dramatic of instances of community support occurred during 1968 when the citizenry approved a bond issue of $1,740,000 to modernize the camp facilities.

Educators in many school systems increasingly express the belief that San Diego's is an outdoor education program that should be replicated in schools over the nation and, so that the public may be informed in detail, a grant was made by the Foundation for the research and writing preliminary to the issuance of this publication. An added reason for our wishing to encourage the reading of the book is that the story, in itself, is of great appeal, combining accurate reporting, sound child psychology, and pedagogy with a delightful style of writing and with illustrations equally effective and charming. One of the several persons who read the manuscript said of it: "Anyone who loves children will love this book," and we believe every reader will share this reaction.

W. K. Kellogg Foundation
Battle Creek, Michigan

# AN EDUCATOR'S PREFACE

WILBUR SCHRAMM has told the story of outdoor education as it is. He has told it in such a moving style that I choked up several times as I read his fascinating script. Parents and teachers alike will be moved by this book's text and pictures.

For me, this book by Schramm could well be one of the more significant publications on education to appear in my lifetime. It could have been done only by one who is both a professional journalist and a professional educator, and, in addition, by one who feels deeply the joy and tragedy of humanity.

I recall vividly the early impetus to "school-out-of-school" education provided by the W. K. Kellogg Foundation. Thirty-five years ago, the Foundation worked with school districts in Michigan to test the theory that city school children would both learn from and enjoy a week of living in a wilderness camp. Here they would study nature — not out of printed books — but out of the real things they see and hear and taste and smell and feel. "What kind of animal made these tracks in the snow?" "Did a forest fire kill all these trees?" "I never knew all these tiny plants and animals could live in this little pond!" "I know now how hard the Indians had to work to make an arrowhead out of this black stone." "Do you see all of these beautiful stars in tonight's heavens?" "Did you see what a good sport our teacher is when we had to clean up the dining room?" "How can we tell how long those bones may have been buried in this river bottom?"

The testing of this theory of learning in Nature's wilderness proved so successful that the Kellogg Foundation funded a national conference in the 1940s, with the Michigan State Department of Public Instruction serving as host. To this conference came many, including a representative from the City and County of San Diego where they had recently started such a program. The knowledge and inspiration gained at the conference aided San Diego officials to crystallize their outdoor education planning. This included the naming of Edwin E. Pumala, who had gained valuable experience in Foundation camping programs, to the directorship of the camps in San Diego County, and this highly qualified man subsequently has guided the California program for more than twenty years.

By arranging for the writing and publication of this volume describing the program, the Foundation has made all of us richer:

- Parents can herein feel much of the thrill and concentration their youngsters undergo as they learn to live and work and discover with their age mates.
- Teachers can understand in vivid paragraphs what educational theorists are telling us about the discovery approach to learning.
- Conservationists will be pleased to know how our schools (over 2,000 school districts across the nation) are using school camps to guide our young to an understanding and appreciation of the beauty and the survival value of nature in balance.
- School board members, recreational council members, and officials and laymen in general, will be encouraged to know that "classroom-out-of-doors" schooling can be successfully launched and maintained without external financial assistance.

The important lesson to be learned from what Schramm has written is that the classroom-out-of-doors can be achieved by any local community that understands the significance of the venture, desires these experiences for its young, and harnesses its resources under inspired leaders and with competent professional staff.

Paul R. Hanna,
*Lee L. Jacks Professor of*
*Child Education Emeritus,*
*Stanford University*

# AUTHOR'S INTRODUCTION

THE PEOPLE OF SAN DIEGO CITY and San Diego County have done a remarkable thing for their children. While the rest of us are laying down more and more asphalt in our cities, and looking at the world more and more through the mass media, they are transporting whole classrooms of children for a week to the mountains and forests, where nature can be seen, touched, studied, and loved, much as it was when the first settlers came to California.

This is more than a camping program. San Diego maintains school camps so that it can have camp *schools*, which are treated as an integral part of a child's studies. On weekends and in the summer, when schools are not meeting, other groups use the camps. This program of outdoor education has built up an uncommon level of loyalty and support in the community. For 22 years, *For ... years* despite financial crises, political changes, a grand jury investigation, and competition for resources, the people of San Diego City and County have determinedly supported the program so that this kind of experience would be available to their children. More than 250,000 boys and girls have passed through the program, and some of the early graduates are now sending *their* children to camp.

I wanted to find out what kind of experience this really is. What kind of teaching goes on when a classroom is transported from the city to the forest? What happens to the children as a result of that experience? What does it require in financial support, leadership, and organization? And in this day of expanding cities and neglected conservation, what does such a program mean to a community? I went to the camps skeptically, and came back—well, in the following pages I have written what I saw.

This is not a fictionalized account. I have described a week in camp as accurately as I could, with the aid of notebook, tape recorder, and camera. And it is only fair to say that, while this narrative is limited to a week in camp, I had to go back several other times in order to understand all that was going on, and talk to more people than could be seen in a week. I spent a number of additional days in San Diego, trying to understand how the supporting organization of the program works, and what the community thinks of outdoor education.

Without the help, advice, and tolerance of many persons, this story could not have been told. I am deeply indebted to the W. K.

Kellogg Foundation, which made the writing possible, and especially to Horace B. Powell, Director of Publications for the Foundation; to Paul Hanna of Stanford, who was friend and aider; to James Reid, of Stanford and Missouri Universities, who also lived a while with the San Diego program and who made the tape recordings for some of the interviews in this volume; to Edwin Pumala, Director of Camping, and Denver C. Fox, Principal of the Camp Schools, who guided me into the intricacies of the program; to Harry Bryce, Head Counselor, and his entire staff at Camp Cuyamaca, Warren Brown and his staff at Camp Marston, and John Craine and his staff at Camp Palomar, all of whom without self-consciousness and always in good temper allowed themselves to be observed and questioned; to a group of civic leaders and school officials in San Diego, many of them named in this book, who talked to me of the past and present of the program and their hopes for its future; and to Linda Miller, who mediated between a rather difficult manuscript and a typewriter.

This book should, in all justice, be dedicated to the people of San Diego City and County, for what they have done in creating and supporting this program. I like to think that, if San Diego children are as uncommunicative with their parents as my own children are with me, this book may answer some long-unsatisfied questions for San Diego parents concerning "what really happens at camp." I hope so. And I hope other parents, other cities, other schools contemplating an outdoor education program will be reading over the shoulders of San Diego. I have tried to write the book so that these potential users of outdoor education could see not only what it is like, but also something of how it is done, and what lies behind the smooth-running program at the mountain camps. Readers who are interested in "what happens at camp" will find the first parts of the book more interesting; readers who are more concerned with the organization will be especially interested in the last three chapters.

Please do not be misled. There is no crime in this book to be traced back through layers of mystery to its perpetrator. There are no good guys to be separated from the bad guys. There are no gunshots. Still I must say that what I saw happening at Camp Cuyamaca, Camp Marston, and Camp Palomar, was very exciting.

W. S.

# TABLE OF CONTENTS

"I had forgotten how much fun it was to hike in mountain air."

# I
## THE OUTDOOR EXPERIENCE BEGINS

AT 9:54 ON A SPRING MORNING, a Greyhound bus, laden with bedrolls, suitcases, and school children, turned off California Route 79 at the Camp Cuyamaca sign. In second gear, the bus eased around the curves of the narrow camp road, and the children looked curiously over the pines and live oaks and down a slope lined with chaparral toward the mountain stream beside which they were going to spend the next five days.

At the same moment, the staff of Camp Cuyamaca (which everyone pronounced Kwee-ya-*Mack*-a) was preparing itself for their arrival. The maintenance men had been up since shortly after 7:00, checking things over. The cooks were in the kitchen by 8:00 preparing to satisfy nearly 200 mountain appetites three times a day, starting at 11:30 that morning. The chief counselor had arrived before 8:30, and the camp teachers appeared between 8:15 and 9:00 in transportation that varied from a pickup truck to a red Porsche. By the time I got to Camp Cuyamaca, about 9:10, a camp teachers' meeting was well under way in the staff lounge.

The subject was rattlesnakes. The California sun had finally won out over a long cold winter, the snow had retreated to the higher peaks and the deep forests, and rangers were reporting that the snakes were coming out of their winter sleep. "We've never had a rattlesnake bite at Cuyamaca," the head counselor was saying as I came in, "but that's because we've been careful — and maybe lucky. This is the most dangerous week. Let's review what we do about these snakes if we meet one."

The head counselor was called Harry. Everything at Camp Cuyamaca seemed to work on a first-name basis. His full name was Harry Bryce. He was a man about 50, heavy-set, round-faced, wearing a plaid wool shirt. I learned later that he had been assistant track coach at Syracuse before the war. He saw California on his way to the Pacific, returned later as a Naval officer, and went into camp work. From the conversation he was directing I learned almost more about rattlesnakes than I cared to know. For one thing, they don't always rattle. How do you know them, then? The flat triangular head is the best sign. If a child is bitten and you don't see the snake, look at the bite, one of the older counselors advised. If the bite is a semi-circle, the snake wasn't a rattler. If it is one or two punctures, you have to assume it was a rattler, and treat it accordingly. A rattler can strike one-third to one-half its length. It is frightened of man, and will retreat unless cornered. The best way to provoke a strike is to make a quick move. I gathered there was a camp rule that whenever a child or a teacher sees a snake, he calls "Freeze!", and the whole group stands still while the teacher takes stock of the situation.

Harry asked the nurse what a victim of rattlesnake bite looked like. The nurse's name was Carol. She was a quiet, serious girl, no taller than many of the children for whom she was to care, but mature and competent. She went over the list of symptoms—pain, sweating, discolored skin, shortness of breath, nausea, faintness, dimmed vision, rapid pulse, shock. The 15 staff members paid close attention; this meeting was obviously of more than academic interest to them. They were seated in casual postures on the sofas and imitation leather chairs of the staff lounge, a few of them on the floor. The room itself was about 20 by 25 feet. A small alcove was lined with bookshelves. In the center of one wall was an old upright piano, and close beside it a somewhat beaten-up dart board. A deer's head, decorated with sunglasses and a red scarf, looked down benevolently on the meeting.

The assistant head counselor, who seemed to be named Walt, led a combined skull practice and demonstration. Walt was a man in his 40's, weatherbeaten and nail-hard. He had come into outdoor education by way of teaching and then the forest service (I learned later) and looked as though he would be a good man behind an axe. As he talked on, I began to realize that there was an enormous difference between preparing to face a rattlesnake alone, and facing it when one is responsible for 20 or 25 children. Walt checked off the steps: Be sure the snake-bite kits are in the field first-aid kit. Take care of the victim first. Put someone else in charge of the other children, and send them a little distance away. Then, when you have time, make a map of the location and send them back to camp for help. But the first job is to treat for shock and get the venom out!

He took a snake-bite kit apart and demonstrated it. It was a simple thing, about three inches long and an inch thick, containing a kind of rubber band, a blade, a vial of antiseptic, and a rubber suction cup. The idea was to cut into the fang marks, and use the cup to suck out the venom. Walt demonstrated on the shapely leg of a girl counselor sitting beside him. "If you ask why I use this leg, it's because it's here, and in shorts," he noted with a nonprofessional wink.

One young man asked whether the old reliable method of sucking out the venom wasn't better. "What if you have a sore in your mouth?" someone else objected. "Oh, well, only one out of ten adults dies from rattlesnake poison," said the nurse, dead-pan.

To kill a rattler, use a long stick and cripple him with a quick blow on his back near the head, Walt advised. But don't follow him, he said; above all, don't pursue him into the bush. Be sure to carry your long sticks when you're on a hike, Harry said. Several of these sticks were standing in the corner. They were about five feet long, with a triangular metal fork on the end. The fork is to pin a snake down when he has been incapacitated, explained Walt. Pin his head down with the forked stick, cut off his head, and bury it 12 inches deep.

Harry began to talk about other matters. It appeared that the week was going to bring problems of another kind. Instead of the usual complement of about 150 children, they might have 175. Some of the schools had been forced to postpone camp trips earlier in the year and were trying to schedule them before school closed. So the dormitories would be crowded, the classes would be larger than usual, and the dining hall would be full. In addition, the information that had come from the schools indicated that there would be an unusual number of behavior problems among this week's campers. I could see from the look the teachers exchanged that this would be no treat for them. They studied lists of children who were to come, and talked about assignments.

"Bus is here!" someone called from the front of the building, and the teachers dashed out to meet it. I followed somewhat more slowly. The staff lounge was on a hillside, overlooking a cluster of dark barracks-type buildings on the flat land beside the stream. I followed down a leafy path, feeling the sun warm on my shoulders and the wind crisp on my face and hands, and came out of the woods on the flat land just in time to see the second and third Greyhound buses pull in.

The children, I knew, had brought their camp gear to school by 8 o'clock or soon after. There had been a great stowing away of sleeping bags, bedrolls, and suitcases, final words of admonition and farewell, and then the buses pulled away about 8:30 with the children waving from the windows and the mothers from the curb. The buses had rumbled up the freeway, through the morning traffic, out of the suburbs, away from the ocean into the dry country, while the scenery browned, sage and cactus appeared in the fields, the road narrowed from six lanes to four, and four to two, and finally came mountain grades and curves. They had turned off interstate route 80 to route 79, then off 79 on the Cuyamaca road. Now they were four thousand feet higher than they had been an hour ago. The bus door had closed on the warm, moist, salty air

"Bus is here!"

of San Diego; now it opened on a crisp, dry mountain breeze that blew with authority. I could see the children in the front of the bus putting on their jackets.

As soon as the doors opened, a camp teacher came aboard. The teacher who climbed on the bus nearest me was a thin tanned young man, with horn-rimmed spectacles and receding hairline. "Welcome to Camp Cuyamaca!" he said.

He was met with a buzz of greetings, talk and laughter, questions and comments. He grinned, held up one hand, and stood silently, hand up, until the bus quieted. "It's a camp custom," he said — "hands up, mouth closed. You shift your vocal mechanism out of gear. Try it." Forty hands went up. Forty-one, to be exact. A boy with a red turtle-neck sweater, who seemed to be a bit of a clown, was holding up both hands. But the bus was quiet.

"We're glad to have you here this week," the teacher said. "I'm Ernie. We all have name tags; you'll get one to wear, too. That teacher down there is named Isabel. He pointed to a very pretty girl in a yellow sweater. He told them to get off the bus, left-side seats first. Boys with him, girls with Isabel.

They climbed off, poured off. I had forgotten how much difference there is in the size of children in the same grade. Many of them were little boys and girls small enough to hold on one's lap. A few of the boys were tall, lanky fellows, who, given a year or two and 30 more pounds, would be playing tackle on the high school football team. The girls, on the average, looked bigger and older than the boys. Some of them were quite mature, and these tended to collect in twos and threes for a little private giggling. The children came off the buses in red coats and white coats, blue shirts and plaid shirts, orange trousers and blue jeans, college girl sweaters and New York Yankees jackets. The modal costume was a sweater or heavy shirt under a short heavy jacket. Both boys and girls wore trousers. Some of them wore hiking shoes, some of them white Beatle boots, and a few, canvas tennis shoes.

"Can I . . .?" asked a girl.

"Yes, we're going to take you right down to the toilets," said Isabel. She had a little of the South in her voice.

"Where are the wild animals?" asked a boy.

"Where can I get my money refunded?" asked the little clown with the turtle-neck.

"You don't want to go home?" I said in surprise.

"Gosh, no," he said. "I don't want to."

"What did you do on the way up?" I asked him.

"Sang a lot," he said. "Some of the kids played cards. Just looked."

They stowed their gear beside the road, and moved down to the toilets in two straggling lines, led by camp teachers. Twenty minutes later they were back, seated on folding chairs in a long, rather dark building which I noticed was called "Hall of the Winds." While they waited for the fourth bus, they sang. Walt, the assistant head counselor, and Dottie, a tall slim blonde teacher, led the songs. They liked action songs and rounds. They boomed out the chorus of a camp song they seemed to have learned beforehand: "I like the mountains, I like the chaparral." As the children from the fourth bus filled in the seats at the back of the room, they all sang "Tell me why the stars do shine," sweet clear sopranos blending with husky adolescent voices that would soon be bassos, and then Harry came to the front of the room to talk to them.

He looked at them, 165 of them. Not all the expected 175 had turned up. They looked at him: a big, plumpish, cheerful-looking man with bright red lumberjack shirt. He held up his hand. They held up theirs. Most of them. They became quiet.

"First, I would like to welcome you to Cuyamaca," he said in a loud, clear, pleasant voice. "Many of our boys and girls who come up don't realize that the school has been here for over 20 years, and that many of the boys and girls who have been here for the school week in the past have grown up and sent their own children to Cuyamaca. Many of them have become teachers and brought their own sixth-grade classes back here. Many of them have become doctors and lawyers. Some of them are in politics. In San Diego, one of our councilmen, Mike Shaeffer, used to be a sixth grader at Cuyamaca. We hope that you will share one week of outdoor education with as much pride as did the boys and girls who have done so in the past.

"I think you will find many opportunities for learning, for making new friends, and, as you know, this week we have two schools up here and that will give you an opportunity to step out of your way and not only enjoy the boys and girls from your own school, but also walk up to a person you haven't met before and say, 'My

"I like the mountains, I like the chaparral!"

name is So and So. I go to this school. What is your name? What school are you from?' Something of that sort."

"My name is So and So," whispered a boy in front of me to his companion. This class seemed to have more than its usual complement of clowns. But there was very little whispering.

"During this week," said Harry, "you will be responsible for many things. Sharing the work load in the dining hall and in your cabin. Many areas of conservation. Many of the activities. We hope you will not turn your back on these things. I think you will have fun, too, along with your learning. I think you will have some exciting new adventures, and many opportunities to become acquainted with the forest, and the part that you can play in maintaining this wilderness area that is one of the most beautiful areas of our country."

Harry glanced down at a sheaf of papers in his hand.

"Now, our first business at hand," he said, "will be to call you by cabin assignments, or dormitories. These names have come up from your schools, and we have divided them. They came up last week. As I call your names will you answer to your names and walk over with your cabin group. I'll call Southwind first."

He paused a minute to explain. "You know our cabins are called Northwind and Southwind for the boys, Eastwind and Westwind for the girls. Cuyamaca is an Indian word for 'meeting place of the winds.' We have an infirmary where our nurse is located, called *Ill* Wind. We have a place where we eat called Mixing of the Winds. This building where we are now is the Hall of the Winds. We also have a building called East Breeze. And many years ago when we had a place where you could buy a toothbrush or a penny post card—those have gone with the wind, too!" he added with a smile—"in the back of this building we had a place called Trade Winds. So the winds have had their full share of the history of Cuyamaca. But lest I become too windy . . ." They laughed. They enjoyed Harry.

"Another word about the nurse and Ill Wind," he said. "During this week we will ask you to take some responsibility for your own personal comfort and safety, and for your health. The nurse is here to see that you do not get ill if it is at all possible. But we cannot follow you about and know if you do not feel well. So it is your responsibility to let us know if you have a headache or a stomach upset. Let your Cuyamaca teacher know about it so we can get you to the nurse. Probably she can take care of you so you will not have to go home. Because we do not have a holding hospital, we can only take care of you for certain small illnesses. If you have an elevated temperature or something more serious, we must call your parents and have them come and take you on down. So don't hesitate to let us know when you don't feel well.

"Now, I'll call your names," he said. "I might mispronounce them, and if I do please pronounce your name correctly. Not everybody. I don't want the whole group to tell me. Just the person whose name I call."

He read the names. Once he read Patrick for Patricia, and was blushingly corrected. He asked for help with a Slavic name. The children gradually sorted themselves out into four groups and moved behind four camp teachers out of the dusk of the Hall of the Winds into the leafy sunshine of the Cuyamaca quadrangle.

Northwind and Southwind stretched along one long side of the quadrangle, opposite the Hall of the Winds. Eastwind and Westwind were at the two ends. All were unmistakable in their architecture and their origin—CCC barracks from the 1930's. I stood in the quadrangle with the 165 other newcomers to Cuyamaca, and watched a large bird with a spot of red swoop over the camp.

I hadn't known just what to expect at Camp Cuyamaca. I had come because some of the people who know most about camping and outdoor education, like Emory Morris of the Kellogg Foundatin and Paul Hanna of Stanford, had insisted that I should. "There are plenty of camps," Paul told me, "but only a few of them have really found out how to pick up a school and move it for a week out of the asphalt and into nature. These city kids go to the mountains with their teachers, and all at once geography, geology, biology, and conservation come to life for them. When they go back, they have their eyes open to things around them, and nature is never again just something to read about in James Fenimore Cooper."

"It's been fabulously successful," said Emory. "San Diego is one of the places that have found out how city and county, schools and government, can work together. They haven't had an easy time with financing, but they have always been able to manage it, because the community believes in it. Everything today is moving toward more and bigger cities, but San Diego is bringing school to the mountains and forests. One of these days you will have one solid city from San Francisco to the Mexican border, and then this pattern for bringing nature back into the lives of boys and girls is going to be priceless."

So I had read into the history of the San Diego camps. The idea seemed to have been born as early as 1941. A City-County Camp Commission had been formed in 1943 to try to lease one of the old Civilian Conservation Corps camps in the middle of Cuyamaca State Park. Apparently it hadn't been easy to persuade the Park Commission; they had looked on the proposal as just another raid on park land. It took the support of influential people as diverse as Leo Carrillo, the actor, and Governor Earl Warren to pass enabling legislation and get the lease signed. That is the way the old CCC campsite became Camp Cuyamaca.

It was used first as a summer recreational opportunity for disadvantaged boys. About 1945 San Diego began to revise its ideas of what a camp should be and do for children. What if it were used not only in the summers, but all year? What if it were used, not only for disadvantaged children but for all children? What if it were used, during the school year, not chiefly for recreation but for learning? That idea brought the schools strongly into the program, and they have played a major part in it ever since. It brought in new leadership, too. The first leaders in the camping program had been oriented toward social welfare and recreational camping; they were succeeded by persons whose backgrounds were in education, especially outdoor education. The first of these was Edwin Pumala. He had worked for the Kellogg Foundation in their camping program, and happened to land in San Diego as a commander in the Coast Guard. San Diego city leaders "hi-jacked" him off his ship, one of them told me with amusement, and made him director of camping and executive director of the camp commission, positions he has held for more than 20 years. The second of the new type of leaders was Denver Fox, who came in as principal of Camp Cuyamaca, became principal of all the camps, and for 20 years has been chief architect of the developing instructional program.

The first classes had moved into Camp Cuyamaca, for a week of school in the mountains, on St. Patrick's Day, 1946. The classes have been coming ever since.

The program soon outgrew Cuyamaca, however, and now there are three camps, soon to be four. In addition to Camp Cuyamaca, an old CCC location was taken over on Mount Palomar, near the great observatory; and a YMCA camp about halfway between Cuyamaca and Palomar has been leased for the school year. These are Camp Palomar and Camp Marston. When I was there, arrangements were being made to lease another private camp, near Marston, at least temporarily.

Altogether more than 250,000 children have used the three camps. Every sixth-grade child in San Diego county, whose school participates in the program, has a chance to spend a week at camp during the school year. His school program is so arranged that what he does in school blends into what he learns in camp, and after he goes home his camp experience is used in his classes. His classroom teacher usually comes to camp with him, and the camp staff is made up of certificated teachers, specially trained in outdoor education. In other words, the camps are not vacations from school; they are extensions of school. "And observe some of the teaching up there," Paul Hanna had said to me. "I think you'll find it rather special."

So that is why I shared a sunny spot in the Cuyamaca quadrangle on that Monday with 165 sixth graders, 15 camp teachers, and a red-tailed hawk. I wanted to see how it actually worked, and, if so, what it took to make it work. What happens when sixth-grade classes are moved bodily from homes and city classrooms to a CCC barracks in the mountains? What happens when you put a lively boy down in fishing and climbing country and try to teach him some geology? How do you teach him from a textbook consisting of trees, rocks, sky, and animals? Is it really a meaningful experience? And what kind of program and organization and staff and support does it require? Those were questions I wanted answered. That is why I was there.

## II
## A LESSON IN DEMOCRATIC LIVING

AN ORIENTATION, I always thought, was a chance to look at the map and get located. It was a meeting where they told you the facts straight, or a chance to find out which way was what. And I guess that's what happened at the Camp Cuyamaca orientation. But I bet it wasn't what any of us new arrivals expected, and the compass didn't turn out to be pointed in the direction we thought it would be.

"What happens next?" I had asked Harry as he bustled out of the Hall of the Winds, enrollment lists still in his hands. "Orientation," he said, hurrying along as he talked. "Medical inspection. They get settled in their cabins. Hear an orientation: It sets the tone for the week."

So I followed a camp teacher whose name tag said "Roy," as he guided his little flock of boys across the quadrangle toward Northwind. Roy was a husky, deeply tanned young man, apparently in his 30's, with a quick smile and the relaxed alertness of a woodsman. He gathered his flock in front of Northwind. The bird with the spot of red sailed out of the pine trees and zoomed upward in the sun.

"What's that?" asked a boy in a black leather jacket.

Later I remembered the exchange that followed, because it was, in miniature, a forecast of so many other discussions I heard at the school camps.

Roy didn't answer his question directly. He said, "Anybody know what kind of bird that is?"

Nobody did, but a roly-poly boy winked and suggested, "F-104?"

"Not bad," said Roy. "He's not supersonic, but he's fast. Maybe he's a pursuit ship, too. Can you see anything about him that indicates he might pursue and catch things?"

"Just that he flies so fast," said a tall boy.

"That's good," said Roy. "But look at him carefully. Here he comes now. Look at him hard!"

"Big claws!" cried a boy.

"Good," said Roy. "Notice anything else?"

"He has a big, sharp beak, hasn't he?" asked the tall boy.

"Right," said Roy. "So he can fly fast, and he's big, and he has the equipment to grab things when he catches them. Now, what do you suppose he might pursue?"

They guessed he might pursue small animals, and Roy said yes, that was his diet. Now, what kinds of big birds are there around here that catch small animals? It wasn't an eagle, they decided; it must be a hawk. "Anybody know what kind of hawk?" asked Roy. He called their attention to the spot of red, and said it was called a red-tailed hawk. "I tell you," he said, "we have a real good bird book here. Let's try to remember to look at it this afternoon or this evening, and look at some of the kinds of hawks there are."

Those two minutes didn't seem very significant to me at the time, but they should have tipped me off to the kind of teaching I should expect at the school camps. I remember thinking at the time that he could have told them right away it was a red-tailed hawk and saved a lot of effort. I didn't realize until later why he hadn't done so. But at that moment I was interested in what happened in an orientation session and not thinking particularly about teaching.

With his level, outdoorsman's gaze, Roy looked over the 46 boys who were to live in Northwind. "I think you're kind of excited," he said, "and that's good. But you aren't so excited that we aren't going to make the best use of our time up here, are you?" He told them to go inside, get a seat pad, and make a circle on the floor in the center of the room. "Why a seat pad?" he asked. "Because sometimes we pick up splinters from the floor, and once you get a big one in your posterior extremity you never ask that question again."

Inside, the young men of Northwind sat in a circle, some with legs crossed, some leaning against the beds with legs out straight in front of them, others with legs drawn up and chins pillowed on their knees. The room was a typical tar-paper barracks, with double-decker bunks along both walls. It was well lighted with electricity, and spotlessly clean. Down at one end of the room were doors opening into communal toilet and shower rooms.

Roy sat in the circle. "I'm very pleased with what I've seen so far," he said in his quiet way. "I think we're going to have a good week."

He looked around at them. "When we sat down, I asked you to sit beside a stranger — a person you didn't know yet. Now, I'm not going to check to see whether you did, but I wonder if you did." He was in a circle of guilty faces.

"The world is full of strangers," he said. "How do we get away from having strangers all around us? What's the best way to eliminate strangers?"

"Make friends?" said a bright-faced little boy with a green-grey plaid shirt.

"Make friends," said Roy. "Get to know them. This is one thing we'll be doing this week. Now, how can we go about making these friends?"

The answers came out: Bunk with them. Do something with them. Be nice to them. Talk to them.

Roy nodded his head in agreement after each answer, but he was looking for still another answer. "How does your dad make friends with strangers?" he asked. "How do most of the men you know make friends with people they don't know? I bet you'll know, but do you want me to show you?" He rose and beckoned to a boy across the circle. "Will you come over here?" Roy offered the boy his big hand. "My name is Roy. What's yours?"

"Joe."

"I'm glad to meet you, Joe. Now, the handshake is pretty important, isn't it?" (The boys made sounds of agreement.) "It's something that our culture has accepted as the way of making friends. Now I've made a friend for today. How about you doing the same? Wouldn't you be interested in knowing the first and last names of a boy you didn't know when you got here this morning?"

He didn't assign them to do it, or tell them he would check up on them, but seemed to be asking them whether *they* didn't think they should. I was a little surprised at that until I began to understand what was going on in the orientation session.

"For those of you who haven't learned my name yet, my name is Roy. You'll be calling us by our first names this week."

"Now let's talk about camp," he said. "What do you expect to get out of camp this week? Why did you come?"

"Have fun and learn," said a boy in the far shadows.

"Get to know the forest," suggested another.

"Get out of school" — hesitantly.

Roy chuckled. "Say that real loud so we all can hear."

The boy said it loud and clear, and everyone laughed appreciatively.

Roy drew out a few more suggestions—come back and see the place again; I want to see the mountains, and the like.

"We'll probably get a chance to do all these things, and more," he said. "But I'm not sure you know a great deal about the camp yet. Perhaps you'll be interested. I heard one of the comments when you walked in here: 'We're in the wrong place—this is an army barracks.' Well, strangely enough, whoever said that was very observant and almost accurate. The roof over our heads was built by the federal government around 30 years ago, and they haven't done much to it since, as you can see. This cabin used to be one of the cabins the Civilian Conservation Corps boys lived in. Now, this was back during the depression that I am sure you have heard your grandfather and grandmother, and maybe even your parents, talk about." (I began to feel older and older.) "After the second World War, it began to be used by the school camps, and slowly, gradually, the program that you are a part of this week was built up. It might not look like much to you, but it's home. This week. And I'm kind of curious to know how differently you'll feel about leaving it Friday than about coming into it today."

He asked them what questions they thought of when they moved into a new home. The answer came—where do we sleep? where do we eat? and so forth—but they came slowly. Roy had to work hard to draw them out. I didn't know whether the trouble was that the boys were still too new in the camp life and shy about talking, or whether they were holding back to look the situation over. I judged there might be some of the latter. In particular, I noticed that one lad with a scornful, handsome face never answered, but some of the other boys looked toward him, as though for his reaction, when *they* spoke.

"You know what I wish," said Roy, after working especially hard to get general participation in the discussion. "I wish we had a great big firecracker. I'd light it and throw it right in the middle of the floor, and it would go

BANG!!"

The boys jumped, and laughed.

"I'm not sure you're quite awake," he said. "We've only had five or six boys doing all the talking. Do they speak for all of you?"

"No." "Sometimes."

"I don't think so," said Roy. "It seems to me that almost every boy here has some ideas, and if he doesn't get in his two cents worth, then he's just letting somebody else speak for him.

"This may be different and strange to you," Roy said. "I doubt that any of you has lived with 40 other boys. Right? So it's new to you. And because it's new, we had better do some planning. Now, do we have any standards to apply to this new situation?"

"Be courteous and obey the rules," said the bright-faced little fellow.

"How do we know that's a good standard for here?" Roy asked. "And we don't have any rules yet, do we? Let's look at it this way: What kind of problems are we likely to have here this week?"

Silence.

Roy smiled. "A whole week without problems, eh? No problems at all. That's good. But let me ask you to do this: Sit where you are, and quietly look around this cabin for 30 seconds. Imagine 45 boys in here. Not sitting quietly on the floor, but living here. What are some of the things that might happen?"

"We might have an argument over who's going to get which bunk."

"Well, if it rains, the roof might leak."

"If you went out, we might have a big pillow fight!"

The boys laughed. Roy, too.

"Only if I go out?" Roy asked. "Anything else you can see that could cause problems? Well, let's work on these," Roy said.

"This bed right here you boys are leaning against: This is the counselor's bed. Each night, there will be a counselor stay here with you. I won't be here every night, but someone will. Now, in the first place, why do you suppose the counselor will be here? What's the purpose of having the counselor here? Carl?"

"For safety?"

"Whose safety?"

"Ours."

"All right. Any other reasons for the counselor to be here?"

"To control us and tell us what to do."

"Did you all hear that?" asked Roy. "Say it good and loud so we all can hear it."

"Control us and tell us what to do."

The handsome sullen boy smiled a bit.

"Control us and tell us what to do," Roy repeated thoughtfully. "So we'll know what to do. How many of you agree with that?"

Two thirds of them raised their hands.

"Did you notice?" Roy asked quietly. "Where was my hand?"

"Your hand was down!" said a boy wearing a jacket that read New York Yankees. He had the hiccups, so it came out, "Your hand was — hic — down!" but the boys paid no attention to the way it was said. Most of them had not observed that Roy's hand was not up along with theirs.

I think that was the turning point of the meeting. I, too, had wondered why Roy did not tell them the rules and get it over with. Now I began to see that he had no intention of telling them the rules. And gradually it began to dawn on all of us that he was asking the boys to make their own rules.

That, I say, seemed to be the turning point. Thereafter, the discussion came easier, and there was closer attention.

"Why do you suppose I didn't raise my hand?" asked Roy. "Why shouldn't I think that I am here to control you and tell you what to do?"

"You won't tell us what to do *all the time*?"

"No," said Roy. "Any other suggestions?"

"Because we're old enough to take care of ourselves."

Roy stared back at the boy who said that, and there was some self-conscious laughter around the room.

"*Are* you?" Roy asked.

"Hope so," said the lad next to him.

"I hope so, too," said Roy, "because that's the basis we have our program set up on. That every boy here is grown up enough to take care of himself." He let that sink in. "Suppose that one boy here—I'm just imagining this—suppose that some boy here isn't grown up enough to take care of himself. What do you think this group of 45 boys might do about it? It might be any one of you. I can't tell. Yet." (They laughed.) "Suppose that a boy isn't grown up enough to take care of himself? What could you boys do to help him?"

The answers came out more quickly now: help him; show him; help him grow up. "It's hard to know how to help someone grow up, isn't it," said Roy, "but there are lots of things we can do. Let's take an example. Suppose you know your cabin is going to be inspected each day to make sure it's neat and clean. Suppose he doesn't have his bunk neat. Straight and well made. And doesn't seem to know how to do it. What could you do? Would you get mad at him because he's sloppy? What would be a better way?"

They suggested they could show him how.

"There are probably boys in here that haven't had much chance to camp out," said Roy. "Maybe they've never made their own bunks before. If we see somebody who's having difficulty, shall we assume that the problem is they don't know how to do it? And give them a hand?"

Roy said he thought they might be deciding some things, and would need a secretary. He asked them to nominate a good writer, and several of the boys said "Danny." Danny, who had a cowlick over his forehead, and wore grey corduroy trousers and tan sweater, was given a pad and a pencil.

"Let's go back to the other matter that you mentioned earlier," said Roy. "One of you boys said, suppose there's an argument over who gets each bunk. How could we settle that?"

"Give it to the one that asks first," suggested the boy with the Yankees jacket.

"That would be one way. Are there other ways?"

"You could arrange them in alphabetical order."

"Then it's kind of important what name you have, isn't it? And would you be doing, or would I be doing it? Wouldn't you like to figure out a way to do it fairly and all by yourselves?"

"You could pick a number, and then the boys could try to guess it."

"Now, wait a minute," said Roy. "Didn't we say a while ago that most of us would kind of like to take care of ourselves?"

"Yes."

"All right. Then, let's try to think out how you could handle this all yourself, without me getting into it. First of all, what's the problem with the bunks? A bed's a bed. They look just about the same to me. What difference does it make which bed you get? Shall I just say, Jimmy take this one, and George this one, and Bill this one? What difference does it make? Or how about this: Shall I put all the boys under 12 years old on the bottom bunk, and all the boys over 12 on the top bunk?"

They laughed and said that wouldn't do.

"Isn't that what you are kind of wondering about?" asked Roy, "whether you are going to get to sleep up there?"

That was the problem, all right, and they talked a while about how they could distribute the top bunks fairly. Gradually, the idea emerged that they might trade around.

"Boys like yourselves in the past," said Roy, "have decided that since there's a top and bottom bunk, they might trade off. You'll be here how many nights?"

"Five."

"Five?" asked Roy in astonishment.

"Four!" they corrected him.

"What's an even division of four nights?"

They decided that they could trade off, two nights in the top bunks, two in the bottom, and that was a fair way to divide up.

"Now let's get to the matter of your belongings," said Roy. "Where are you going to keep your belongings?"

They looked around. "On the floor under the bottom bunk?" a boy suggested.

"That's where the boys have usually kept them," said Roy. "How did you know that?"

"Seemed like the best place."

"When you looked around for closets, you didn't see any, did you?" said Roy. "And I don't either. But why not keep them out in the middle of the floor?"

"Might come by and trip over it."

"Might kick a hole in it."

"Somebody might be moving around at night, and fall over it and hurt himself."

"So it's for the safety of the cabin, then," said Roy. "Are we all agreed that we have a good safe place to put our belongings? Where is it?"

"Under the beds." The little secretary was writing busily.

Roy raised another problem: how to keep things from getting lost, or just disappearing. They worked that over for a while: put it back in your suitcase when you're through with it, seemed to be the general idea.

"Suppose you want to borrow something," said Roy. "How do you go about it?"

"Ask for it?"

"Do you all agree?"

They did.

"Is there anybody here who feels that if you want to use something you just reach out and grab it?"

"No."

"You ask permission. Will it work that way?"

They agreed it would.

"You see, what we're talking about now are ways of getting along inside this cabin with the least amount of difficulty with each other," said Roy. "If we have particular problems later on, we can come together like this and go over the problems we have. This doesn't have to be the only time we get together. Maybe, as time goes on, we'll want to do this same thing again. And Thursday night we'll get together again, and talk about the week you've spent here at Cuyamaca.

"Now I wonder if there are any other problems you ought to decide about," Roy said thoughtfully. "I was just looking at those rafters — look pretty inviting, don't they?"

"Gee!" said a boy who was wearing a San Diego State College sweatshirt.

"What do you suppose is likely to happen?"

"Somebody's going to climb them."

"Do you think so?"

They did.

"They look almost like parallel bars, and there's lots of them. Do you think it would be wise to climb on them?"

There was disagreement.

"Can you think of any reason why it might not be wise?"

"Somebody might fall and break a leg."

"If you hung too heavy on them, part of the roof might fall in."

"Those are two possibilities," said Roy. "I'm not sure the roof would collapse, but I wouldn't take any chances on it."

They talked about the possibility of getting hurt, or hurting someone else by falling on them.

"If you get an injury, what happens? What has to happen?" asked Roy.

"They call your parents and you go back."

"Of course, that depends on how serious the injury is," said Roy. "Could I see the hands of the boys who still want to spend the week here?"

They were rather astonished. Their hands went up.

"Do you have any guarantee it won't be you that gets hurt?"

"No."

"I can tell you this: You will get your money back for the time you didn't spend here, but you won't get another chance to come up and spend a week. So let's be careful and be safe. Now when we think back to what you said earlier, that you wanted to take care of *yourself*, do you think it's a good idea to be up on those rafters?"

They agreed, and Roy turned the conversation to the danger of splinters — in the feet or fingernails or in what he called the posterior portion. They decided that it would be better to wear shoes in the cabin, and sit on mats when they sat on the floor.

"I was wondering about one other thing," said Roy. "I didn't see any maid get out of the bus this morning. We don't have any janitor here. I wonder who's going to keep this place clean?"

"I guess it's going to be us," said a boy with a worried look on his face.

"Who do you mean, us?" asked Roy. "The boys? The counselors? Who?"

"All of us."

"The boys and the counselors?"

"Just the boys."

"Why do you say that, Mark?" Roy asked. "Why do you say, just the boys?"

"They're the ones who usually dirty it up the most."

The roly-poly boy dissented. "If you would throw that firecracker on the floor," he said, "I think you ought to clean it up!"

Roy joined in the laughter. "I agree that if I dirty the floor like that I ought to clean it up," he said, "but let's talk about it a minute."

They decided that everyone ought to take care of his own belongings, and any special dirt he causes, and that there ought to be teams that would take turns keeping the floor and the shower room clean. Roy sent two boys out to report how many toilets were unflushed, and how many faucets were dripping. They came back with a perfect report, and Roy pronounced it "fantastic!"

"I'm wondering about one other thing," he said. "Just suppose — I don't think it will happen — but suppose we have a little altercation here in the cabin. Suppose there is a little pushing and shoving between two boys. For any reason. How could we go about settling something like that, fairly and squarely?"

They talked it over. Roy turned them firmly away from the idea that the counselor might settle it. "How could *you* handle this?"

he asked. They finally decided that the thing to do would be to pull the boys apart and let them cool off. But still better would be to try to see that no fights start in the first place.

"Is fighting a good way to settle our difficulties?" asked Roy. "Do we ever settle much that way?"

He called on the secretary for a report of what they had decided. The boy read his notes:

"First is, put your suitcase under the bottom bunk. Under your own bunk. Put your belongings in your suitcase, when you're not taking them or something. And ask for something if we want to borrow it. And for two nights sleep in the top one, and then for two nights down in the bottom one. And we're supposed to keep the bathroom clean, and be sure the faucets are shut off and the toilets flushed. And we shouldn't swing on the beams up there — up on the roof. And we shouldn't run on the floors with bare feet. And settle our fights. Try not to have fights."

"Good," said Roy. "Everybody agree with that?"

"What if both boys want to sleep on the bottom bunk, not on the top at all?" someone asked.

"Then we'd expect you to work out some sort of compromise," said Roy. "You see, we have a lot of faith in boys. We think you can handle these problems. And if we have more problems, we can come together and talk about them.

"There are a few things you need to know about the camp that I think I had better tell you now," he said. He explained how fire drill worked in camp, and what the signal sounded like. He pointed out that they were in a state park, and therefore were not permitted to collect anything and take it home with them. They were also not permitted to throw rocks. "There will be people all over this area," he said. "You won't even know where they are. Pick up a rock and throw it over in the bushes and you might get — more than you bargained for." He demonstrated the safe way to climb in and out of upper bunks. "And when you're ready to come down, warn your neighbor below," he advised. "Say coming down! or preparing to descend! or Geronimo! or something.

"If there's any way I can help you, or any of the other counselors can help, come and ask us," he said. "I'm here to help. But you don't want me to be your conscience, do you? You have consciences of your own. We understand each other about that, don't we? Come to me for help, but I hope you won't come for what you ought to be deciding yourself."

He sent them to bring in their suitcases and sleeping bags.

I tried to interpret what I had just witnessed. It had not been what I had expected. I had imagined it would be a briefing, so that

Roy could explain the camp rules and customs. Instead of that, he had tried as hard as he could *not* to tell them the rules—rather, to try to get *them* to make rules they were prepared to live by. Apparently, within certain very broad limits—health, safety, law of land—the school camps were encouraging their campers to take over as much responsibility for their own discipline as they were willing to carry. What I had heard, in the last 40 minutes, was not so much an orientation as it was a lesson in democratic living, without ever mentioning the word democracy.

"What would you have done," I asked Roy when the boys went outside for their luggage, "what would you have done if they had decided that *you* should make the rules?"

"It has happened," he said. "Occasionally we get a group so used to authority that they can't imagine anything else. So I make the rules. Then, after a day or two, when they find they don't like it, we take up the matter again. By that time they are usually ready to accept some of the responsibility."

It occurred to me that I might be seeing a good test of the system. I recalled what had been said at the teachers' meeting about an unusual number of behavior problems among the present campers. I remembered that boy with the scornful face who had never entered into the discussion in Northwind, although so many other boys when they spoke looked at *him*. It would be worth seeing how the invitation to freedom and responsibility worked *this* week.

When the baggage was stowed away and the sleeping bags laid out on the bunks, we lined up outside to go to lunch. I heard the voice of my friend with the turtle-neck sweater: "Where do you get your money refunded?"

"Is that all you know to say?" growled a blonde boy in a quilted jacket.

"Jeez, I'm hungry," said turtle-neck.

We moved up the hill, four straggly lines from four cabins, each led by its respective Moses toward the promised land of the dining hall. The hawk with the spot of red flashed overhead.

# III
# THE DISCOVERY APPROACH TO LEARNING

IT BECAME APPARENT at lunch that starvation was not one of the wilderness perils that need concern me at Cuyamaca.

The dining room was large and airy. There were windows on three sides, fireplace in front, and kitchen service windows at the rear through which white-coated cooks could be seen preparing for the invasion. Boys and girls from the Four Winds streamed into the room, hung their jackets on hooks around the wall, and found seats. They were at tables for eleven—one teacher, ten children. I sat down between two little boys whom I had seen at Northwind, and was politely told to move: boys and girls were alternating at the tables today. So I sat between two golden-haired little girls who said they were from Westwind. "Are you a camp teacher?" one of them asked respectfully. "I'm too old and weak to be a camp teacher," I said. "Oh," they said, less respectfully. "He's a visitor," explained a tall handsome woman who seemed to be the camp teacher at the table. She introduced herself as Edna. "I'm Bill," I said. "I didn't get a name tag." "Bill," said the little girl at my left, "you're sitting on my napkin."

I looked around at 165 excited youngsters. Each had a name tag to represent his individuality in that crowd, but there was

"Starvation was not one of the wilderness perils that concerned us at camp."

nothing that so impressed one, seeing them all together, as the great individuality among them. They were short and tall, plump and thin, honey blondes, raven hair, towheads, crew cuts, long hairs. They wore solid color sport shirts, plaid shirts, sweaters of every color. Many of them wore sweatshirts or jackets with the name of a team or institution. I saw San Diego State, Yale, California, YMCA, Chargers, Green Phantom, U.S. Marines, Notre Dame—oh, yes, and one boy's sweatshirt bore a picture of a bearded man with the name printed below: "Beethoven." It made a colorful dining room, because people in California like to wear bright colors. But the quality that tied them all together was excitement. You could see it in their wide eyes and quick movements, and the way they spoke a little louder than usual. I presumed that few of these children had ever been to camp before; many of them might never have been away from home overnight. Everything that happened today was new, and they had to learn a new set of mores. And so they darted glances around the room and called to their friends at adjoining tables, and Edna said quietly, "Hadn't we better keep our voices down? It gets pretty noisy in here when you call across the room."

Then Harry was at the front of the room. He raised his hand. They raised theirs. The dining hall quieted. He told them about dining hall customs at Cuyamaca: people talked softly so other tables could talk, too, without shouting; each table appointed a few children as "hoppers" to carry plates of food from the kitchen windows; after each meal, three children would clean the table, do the dishes, and set the table again; other children would help sweep out the dining room; they would all take their turns at this, and the camp teacher would explain how.

He introduced the chef Pauline, the cooks, the nurse Carol, and the camp clerk Lois. The camp teachers stood up one by one and introduced themselves: "My name is Walt; I'm going to take some of you on conservation." "My name is Carla; I'm going to be with you in Westwind this afternoon." "I'm Don; I'm looking forward to telling the story of the forest tonight." "My name is Isabel; welcome to camp, boys and girls!"And so on. And then we ate.

Edna appointed two "hoppers," and told them to join a line in front of the kitchen service windows. The direction of the line was indicated by pictures of two small striped creatures, labeled respectively IN-SKUNK and OUT-SKUNK. The hoppers returned bearing enormous platters of baked ham, scalloped potatoes, beans, and apple sauce. Cole slaw, bread, butter, and four cartons of milk were already on the table. The dining room quieted in tribute to the food.

"Bill, you haven't had any milk," said the little girl whose napkin I had sat on, and whose name tag said "Cindy." I judged that was a requirement of a healthy visitor, and poured some.

"Can we have seconds?" asked a boy who was half through his first plateful. "All you want," said Edna. "I wonder if we oughtn't to keep our elbows off the table," she said without indicating any particular elbows. "Sally," she said a minute later, "the meat is all gone. Would you go back and bring us some more?" I wondered whether some of these youngsters were not accustomed to such bounteous meals and were making up for past scarcities. But Sally, in what looked like an I. Magnin blue sweater, had been going after the food just as hard as the girl in the sweatshirt. I ascribed the appetites to mountain air and good cooking. And then there was Pauline, the chef, who beamed from the kitchen on everyone who came back for seconds. It occurred to me that, if I didn't stop overeating, Pauline's good food might prove a greater hazard than snakebites.

Between helpings, I tried to identify the children around my table. The two little girls on either side of me were not from San Diego, they said, but from a school district called La Mesa— Spring Valley, which is between San Diego and the mountains. The father of one of them ran a filling station; the other's father was in the Navy. The boys on either side came from Diego. The boy at the far end of the table was the handsome, sullen lad I had seen in Northwind during the orientation meeting. His name tag said he was "Dan," but he himself said little except out of the corner of his mouth to his neighbors. Toward the other end of the table was a tall, gangly lad in a sweatshirt, who seemed rather withdrawn and self-conscious. John was his name, he said; he lived with his "aunt," which, I gathered, was a euphemism for a foster home. Beyond him sat Maria, also wearing a swirtshirt, who said she lived in San Diego and didn't have a father anymore (I had thoughtlessly asked what her father did), but had a lot of brothers and sisters. She had wonderful dark eyes under long lashes, and a dark Spanish complexion; some day she would be a beauty. On Edna's side of the table Sally in the I. Magnin sweater sat at one end. She said she lived on the north side of San Diego, and her family had a boat. At the other end of the table was a Negro girl with big excited eyes and graceful movements. Between her and Edna was an all-American boy type, with a blonde lock falling over his forehead, a flashing, half-embarrassed smile, and the coordinated moves of an athlete. The other boy at the table

"We had to learn to take care of things ourselves."

was a little fellow who also had been at Northwind. He said he carried papers, and got his tan that way, and had to pay his brother a dollar extra to cover the route this week. He was going to be a scientist, he said. What kind? Well, maybe a molecular biologist. Had he read much about molecular biology? Well, his father worked in that sort of thing, he said. I had forgotten how varied the backgrounds would be in a place like San Diego.

Mealtime was not the occasion for extended conversation. At least, not the first meal. The food was too good, and everybody too hungry. The hoppers brought bread pudding, which Edna ladled into 12 bowls. Later she initiated them into the rites of dishwashing. They washed their hands and then brought pans, one with soap, one with rinse water and disinfectant. Edna scraped together food scraps. "John, you feed Porky," she said. "Maria, you feed Smokey." Porky and Smokey were two cans beside the fireplace. Smokey got the paper napkins and cartons and things that would burn; Porky got the garbage. I tried to help dry dishes. "Have you washed your hands?" Maria asked with reproof in her voice. I slunk away. I had to dodge a team of boys who were pushing wide brooms over the floor. I suspect the mothers of some of these children might have been a bit astonished at the energy their children were putting into clean-up tasks.

There was a bit of quiet time after lunch, and I had a chance to take stock of my schedule. Monday was orientation. Tuesday was field science and crafts. Wednesday was an all-day hike. Thursday was mostly science. Conservation ran through all those three days. Friday was a time to finish unfinished business and get ready to leave. That was the general framework of the program, although the schedule looked more complicated than that because at any given time ten groups of children might be active in ten different things.

I had asked Edna what she had been doing that morning. She had been with the girls in Eastwind, she said. They had settled into their cabin, and had their medical inspection. The nurse had gone to the girls' cabins while the boys were having orientation. After lunch the boys would have medical inspection, and the girls would have orientation. I decided to look in on Eastwind, and see how the girls handled their rule-making problems.

The interior of a girls' cabin looked very much like the interior of a boys' cabin—double bunks, rafters, rather subdued light from high windows, dark walls, and unfinished wood floors. Ellen sat in a circle of girls and ran the meeting in a friendly, no-nonsense manner, sprinkled with humor. The meeting moved more quickly than the boys' orientation; Edna had less trouble than Roy in getting her campers to talk—probably because they had been in camp several hours longer, and had gotten past the initial tenseness and wariness. They had already chosen their bunks, stored their luggage, and felt more securely settled. Then, too, the Northwind boys may have been reflecting more resistance to authority. And it may have been because, as Edna suggested later with a twinkle in her eye, the female of the species is a nobler animal.

In any case, Edna's orientation lasted 25 minutes instead of the 40 Roy had needed, and went over about the same ground. The Eastwind girls had come up for about the same variety of reasons as the Northwind boys. One girl said shyly that she came because she wanted to get away from her sisters, and everyone laughed, but Edna said understandingly, "A little change of pace, eh?" When she asked them who should make the rules for a group like this, the same shy little girl said, "*You* should."

"Do you think the counselors should do it?" asked Edna. "Does anyone have another opinion?"

"All of us," suggested a girl whose name tag said Cecelia.

"You think *all* of us should. Now here we have a difference of opinion? What do you think, Ann?" Edna seemed to be able to peer through the dusk of Eastwind and read a name tag clear across the circle. I could hardly see some of the faces clearly, but Edna apologized when she couldn't make out a name.

"Oh, we could pick a person, you know," said Ann.

"Choose one person in the group to do it?"

"No!" said half a dozen girls.

## CAMP CUYAMACA — DAILY SCHEDULE

| TIME | MONDAY | TUESDAY | WEDNESDAY | THURSDAY | FRIDAY |
|---|---|---|---|---|---|
| 6:45 | | Reveille | Reveille | Reveille | Reveille & pack |
| 7:15 | | Breakfast gong | Breakfast gong | Breakfast gong | Breakfast gong |
| 7:30 | | Breakfast | Breakfast | Breakfast | Breakfast |
| 8:00 8:30 | | Clean up cabins, grounds | Clean up cabins, grounds | Clean up cabins, grounds | Clean up cabins, grounds, bldgs. |
| 8:45 | | Flag raising | Flag raising | Flag raising | Flag raising |
| 9:00 | Staff arrives | Activity meeting (weather) | Activity meeting (animal talk) | Activity meeting | State Park Indian Museum |
| 9:30 | Staff meeting | Conservation Field Science & Ecology Hikes Rocks & Minerals Products of Forest Indian Lore & Geology Wildlife & Tracking | Conservation All Day Hikes: Northward Ho East Mesa Beaver Valley Southward Ho Cuyamaca Ramble West Mesa Stonewall Peak | Conservation Crafts for Tues. conservationists Geology-Ore panning Pond Biology Forest Fire Spotting, Location & Control Space & Light Study Orienteering | Square Dance or Completion of Craft articles Woodquiz Scramble Evaluation |
| 10:30 | Campers arrive | | | | |
| 11:00 | Orientation Nurse visit | Trees of Forest | Indian Camp | Indian Lore | |
| 11:30 | Wash for lunch | End of Activity | End of activity | Wildlife Study | |
| 11:45 | Lunch gong | Lunch gong | | End of Activity | Lunch |
| 12:00 | Lunch | Lunch | | | Song Assembly |
| 12:45 | Nurse visit | Quiet time | Quiet time | Quiet time | Buses depart |
| 1:45 2:00 2:15 | Orientation Beds, baggage, collecting camper money, candy, etc. | Activity meeting (Indian songs) Craft Activity Rocks Dwarf Gardens Clay Plaster Wood | Activity meeting (rainy day) Return from Hikes Monkey Bridge | Activity meeting Outdoor science activities: Geology-Ore panning Pond Biology Forest Fire Spotting, Location & Control Space & Light Study Orienteering Indian Lore Wildlife Study | Cabin check |
| 3:00 | Cabin group exploration to boundaries, Craft shops, Museums Science labs, Camper books | | 4:00 Showers | | |
| Sign up | | 4:00 End of activity 4:15 Showers 4:45 Sign up | 4:30 Quiet Time Sign up | 4:00 Showers | |
| 5:00 | Wash for dinner | | | | |
| 5:15 | Dinner gong | | Campers' | | |
| 5:30 | Dinner | | Birthday | | |
| 6:15 | Roving Interest | | | | |
| 7:00 | Campfire Slide talk Introduction to Forest Community | Indian Ceremony | Cabin Science and Nature Interest, Activity, Astronomy, Star Hikes, Animal Talk | Evaluations — Last Campfire | |
| 8:00 | Bedtime | | | | |
| 8:30 | Lights out Stories — Music | | | | |
| 9:00 | Taps | Taps | Taps | Taps | |

"We could have a committee or something," said Cecelia.

"A committee? What do you think, Margaret?"

"Well, I think each individ — individual girl should think of their own rule. One rule."

"We'd have a lot of rules, wouldn't we?"

"I mean everybody pick a rule, and then pick the better ones."

"Who do you think should pick the better ones?"

"You?"

"Now look," said Edna. "Let's understand each other. Are you saying what you really think? I don't want you to say what you think I want to hear. Say what you really think. The way you want it to be in the cabin this week."

"We could pick some rules and have a vote on them . . ."

"You think it would be a good idea for all of us to choose the rules and decide on them?"

"Uh-huh."

"Why is this better than having just one person decide on them?"

"One person might get what she wants, but the others mightn't."

Obviously, the girls were no more accustomed than the boys to this kind of responsibility, but they worked it out, just as the boys did, and Edna led them through a kind of permissive Socratic dialogue, until, toward the end of the meeting, a pink-cheeked girl named Lorna read out a set of rules she had printed beautifully on her secretary's pad:

> Walk in cabin.
> No jumping on beds.
> No playing in restrooms.
> Walk in shower room.
> Keep cabin clean every day.
> Keep suitcases under beds.
> Keep your clothes together.
> Pick monitors for cleaning.
> Do not be noisy.

"Everybody agree?" asked Edna. "We'll put these up on the door, then. How well you print!" she said to Lorna.

But she wasn't willing to stop the dialogue there. "Suppose you decide you don't like some of these rules," she said, "what do you do about it? Suppose you decide it isn't a good rule. What do you do? Just not follow it? What would be the best thing to do? Denise, what do you think?"

"Well, if you don't agree with one of these rules, you can go up and tell the counselor," suggested Denise. "Then maybe we can pick out another rule."

"What do we mean by *we*? The counselors?"

"The group."

"Oh, the group. Terry?" I don't see how she could possibly read that name across the circle.

"We could, say, sit down and have another talk. Then maybe change the rules to make it work better, or something."

"That's a very good idea," said Edna. "Do you agree? Now, can you do this, this week, all on your own? If there's anything this week that seems to you a problem, can we just sit down and talk about it? If you want to get together like this, just mention it to the teacher, and we'll take time. We'll make time."

Just as in the morning meeting, democracy was never mentioned, and yet clearly the children were being challenged to practice it. And as at the end of the other orientation meeting, I wondered whether it was merely a brave venture, or whether it really worked.

Leaving the girls to post their new rules, I looked in on Northwind again. My first impression, when I walked into the cabin, was that the boys were being frisked. They were giving up their money, chewing gum, candy, pocketknives, and medicines. The medicines were being tagged for Carol the nurse. The other articles were put into envelopes with the boy's name, and put away for safekeeping.

"Why?" the boys were asking, and Roy was joking with them as he explained.

"We had thought some of asking you to give up all your clothes and put you in skins and feathers, and have you look for your own food, the way the Indian boys did when they were here. But after thinking it over we decided to leave you your clothes and your cameras. And feed you. But you can't spend any money up here, and this way you can't lose it either. And you know, maybe by getting rid of some of these other things you use in the city you'll get a better idea of what's important up here!"

The pattern I kept noticing that afternoon and most of Tuesday was the children testing to see how far the camp teachers would let them go. The teachers met the probes calmly and firmly, and, I thought, consistently. They calmed down the noise, and made sure of attention, and did all this with a warmth and understanding that didn't invite hostility. Roy grinned at his 45 boys and told them that the nurse would be in to examine them, in a few minutes. (Protests: Ah, there ain't nothing wrong with me! We aren't sick. Let's get out in the woods!) He grinned again, and held up his hand, and, after a moment, so did they. After the nurse had gone, he said, they would have a little hike. They would tour the camp, and see a little of the country around. And maybe cross the

Monkey Bridge.

That set off a flurry of questions in the midst of which Carol the nurse arrived. She popped thermometers into every available mouth, thereby simultaneously recording temperatures and silencing 45 boys—a tactic which, I assume, the medical profession has perfected through years of experimenting. Looking around the circle of thermometers, Carol talked a little while about accidents. "Watch out for splinters," she said. "The dormitory floor is full of them; wear shoes or slippers when you walk around inside. Outside, watch for poison oak and stinging nettles. Those are nasty; your counselors will point them out to you. If you see a snake, stand still and yell 'freeze!'. Then everybody *freeze*. Let the counselor decide whether it's poisonous or not. We tell you to freeze, because a snake gets frightened and lashes out at quick movements. Stay out of the chaparral; it's hard on your clothes and your skin, and it's a favorite place for snakes. Stay out of the high grass; you can't see a snake there."

She walked over to a big first-aid kit. (I looked inside. There were band-aids, tweezers, an antiseptic, poison oak lotion, chapping cream, a bottle marked for athlete's foot, mentholatum for dry nostrils, scissors, and Kleenex.) "You're welcome to use these," she said. "I am going to take your medicines and keep them for you until Friday, you know. Those of you who have to take medicine every day, we know about; you just come over and I'll give the medicine to you when it's time. But let's don't have any extra bottles or pills lying around here. They might get lost, or somebody might take them by mistake."

She began to collect the thermometers and read them. "If you get to feeling bad," she said, "—if you have a breaking out, or a pain or bad headache, or think you might have hurt yourself with a fall, or feel as though you're coming down with a cold, or have a bad sore throat, come and see me. If you need a doctor, we'll get you one. If it's something we can take care of, we'll take care of it. But don't hesitate to come," she said.

She extracted the last thermometer. "Disgustingly healthy," she said. "Trying to do me out of a job? Was anybody sick last week? Any of you have sick brothers and sisters?" Heads shook all around the circle. "Any questions?" she asked.

"Can we pick up a snake if it's not poisonous?" a boy asked.

"Don't pick up a snake or a lizard unless your teacher says you may," Carol said firmly. "Sometimes you can't always tell at first glance whether a snake is poisonous. Nice cute little baby rattlers are about as deadly as their fathers."

"Their mothers?" said a boy with a twinkle.

"And another thing," said Carol, "don't pick up any lizards unless your teacher tells you to. Some of these little fellows can almost bite your finger off."

"There's a lizard here looks just like a little alligator," said Roy. "Does he live in the water?"

"I've always seen them in the grass," said Roy.

Carol looked around for more questions, picked up her thermometers, and hurried off to her next cabin. I detained her a minute outside the door. "What do you do if you find a kid has a fever?" I asked.

"A few of these boys did," she said. "If it's under 99, I pay no attention to it. If it's between 99 and 100 and there are no other symptoms, I take it again in a couple of hours. We have a lot of spurious high readings here. They're excited, and sometimes they're feeling the altitude. If it's still high after a couple of hours, we do something about it."

"What?" I asked.

"Look for other things," she said. "Pain, breaking out, swelling, sore throat, sickness in the family, and so forth. If I can't find anything, and the temperature is not too high, I keep the child overnight in the infirmary. Otherwise, I decide whether to get the child to a doctor, or call his parents and send him home."

"Where is the nearest doctor?" I asked.

"About half an hour away," said Carol. She hurried toward the next cabin.

The young men of Northwind erupted into the afternoon like wild colts — running, jumping, kicking, turning handsprings, with the sheer exuberance of being 12 years old. Then I saw a man whom I recognized as Denver Fox walking across the quadrangle, and I left them to talk to him.

I was glad to have a chance to talk with the man who has the rather unlikely name of Denver Colorado Fox, because he is one of the historic figures in the school camp story. More than anyone else, for 20 years he has been responsible for shaping the instructional program. He has the sensitive face of an intellectual, the alert, friendly manner of a man who spends his life dealing with people and listening to problems, and the dignified mien of one who carries responsibilities. You might say he looks like a school principal, which he is. And yet the tan on his face and hands, the casual dress and open collar, proclaim him an outdoorsman. I remember thinking at the time that it was appropriate that Denver Fox should wear metal-rim spectacles: devoid of any fanciness; simple, modest, spare, and efficient. They seem to go well with a sharp, clear mind.

We followed Northwind around the camp, while Roy and another counselor named Ernie pointed out the different buildings. Around the main quadrangle, which consisted of the four dormitory cabins and the Hall of the Winds, were a half dozen other old CCC buildings, used variously as woodworking and rock craft shops, maintenance buildings, biology laboratory, storehouses, and the like. One small building held an Indian exhibit—wickiup, cooking area, a collection of cooking jars, flour grinding stones, arrow and axe heads. This was all left by the Diegueno Indians who used to live in that area, Roy told the boys. Cuyamaca was one of their words, and half a dozen of their dwelling sites are still easily recognizable near the camp. At one corner of the quadrangle was Ill Wind, the infirmary, and at the other end was a weather station where, the boys were told, every week a certain

Camp Cuyamaca — "Next year the camp will look entirely different," said Denver.

number of boys and girls would be appointed Weather Birds and taught how to use the instruments and make some predictions. All these were on the flat land beside the creek. The buildings were typical of CCC camps, with roofs that looked brown in the sun, and unpainted walls that were nearly black in the shade and grey in the sunlight.

On the wooded hillside above the flat land were several newer buildings—the large rectangular dining hall, which was in classical State Park architecture, a one-story staff house and an annex, both of which resembled in some ways California tract homes.

"Put all this out of your mind," said Denver. "Next year the camp will look entirely different. Every building you see on the flat—the old, black tar-paper buildings—all those will be gone."

With the back of an envelope and some vivid description he tried to get me to see how the new camp facilities would look. The new buildings were going to be possible because the City and County of San Diego, in a rather remarkable demonstration of confidence, had decided to finance approximately one and a half million dollars worth of bonds to get Camp Cuyamaca and Camp Palomar out of the CCC era. So all the old CCC buildings, with their splintery floors and unfinished walls, would be torn down, and all the cement foundations would be dug up. The flat land would go back to being a beautiful mountain meadow, as it had once been, and the incense cedars would furnish shade around it as they had for the Indians. The camp would move up the hill, into the trees and toward the present dining hall and staff quarters. He diagrammed a neat cluster of buildings—four dormitories, infirmary, dining hall enlarged to serve as a combined dining hall and auditorium, service buildings, small meeting rooms, and the like. The architect had designed the new buildings with earthy colors to blend into the landscape.

The problem in designing a camp like this, he said, is to minimize the feeling of a huge operation—the institutional look, he said, "that makes a child come into a camp of 200 other children and say, My goodness! look at all those people!" To minimize this, he said, the dormitories would be built almost as squares, with four separate living units opening into a main central area which would be the meeting area. Thus, only 12 or 14 boys will be in any one living unit, but at night one camp teacher can supervise all four units. Only when the campers come together in the dining room or auditorium, will they be in really large groups. Any camp like this one, he explained, faces the problem of distributing the very expensive manpower represented in credentialed teachers as efficiently as possible. This means that you want to be able to use as few camp teachers as possible in times of low-organization activities, such as night-time supervision, rest time, cleanup time, and the like, but to be able to put teachers in close touch with pupils in times of high-organization activity like conservation or pond biology. That kind of flexibility is therefore built into the new plans.

While the inhabitants of Northwind hiked up a steep hillside, Denver and I sat on a log and talked about the program I was seeing.

He reminded me, without going into details, how the program was organized. The participating school systems were responsible for the instruction—hiring the teachers and deciding on the content of the program. The City-County Camp Commission (on which the schools were represented, along with the city council, the county supervisors, and the county PTA) was responsible for camp facilities, for general administration, and for coordinating community support and cooperation. The parents, if they could afford to, paid the cost of their children's food, lodging, transportation, and accident insurance, which added up to about 20 dollars per child. The cost of instruction was approximately 22 dollars per pupil. A little over 15,000 sixth graders were going to camp this year, and the number would be 17 or 18,000 in the following year. But he emphasized that another ten thousand children and adults use the camp on weekends and in the summer, for recreational camping, and for special purposes like music camp or safety patrol camp. When the schoolchildren and school camp staff went home on Friday afternoon, he said, the camp buildings and grounds we were looking at would be taken over by a group of approximately 130 campers from San Diego, who would be there until Sunday afternoon.

From where we sat, we could look across the camp to the West Mesa, and see beyond it the big shoulder of Cuyamaca Peak, and the rocky tip of Stonewall Peak. Cuyamaca was the highest mountain in the neighborhood; Stonewall looked as though it would be the most fun to climb. It was not spectacular scenery. It had neither the awesome quality of the high Sierra, the green majesty of the redwood groves to the north, nor the calm endlessness of the deserts farther east. It was typical Southern California mountain scenery—rough stone outcroppings, much chaparral and other low growth, a variety of oaks, pines, and cedars, rather than a forest of one kind of tree. The camp itself was in a mountain meadow beside a small stream, between two mesas. Green, grey, and brown alternated over the landscape. Despite its roughness, there was something pleasant and peaceful about it.

I asked Denver about the other camps, which I hoped to see something of while I was in the mountains. He said they were all within about 40 miles, as the crow flies. When I climbed a little higher, he said, I could see a line of three mountains—Cuyamaca Peak, Middle Peak, and North Peak. Camp Cuyamaca was on the lower slopes of Cuyamaca, to the southeast. Camp Marston was on the slopes to the northwest of North Peak. Then beyond some plateau land to the north was another range, the Aqua Tibia mountains, with Mount Palomar rising to a little over 6,000 feet. Camp Palomar was in the state park on the side of Mount Palomar. All the camps were between 4000 and 5000 feet above sea level.

So far as the programs are concerned, he said, a youngster going to one camp would get about the same basic kind of experience in relating to other people, exploring the out-of-doors, learning to solve problems, that he would get in either of the other camps. The program is not a complete carbon copy, though, because each camp tries to capitalize on the potential of its site. Marston is close enough to the desert to be able to make use of that. Palomar is close to the observatory, and therefore builds part of its program around that. I would notice at a camp like Marston, he said, that there were many small living units, holding 10 to 14 children each, in contrast to the large ones at Cuyamaca that housed 40 to 50 children together. Camp Marston, therefore, has to put special emphasis on building up pride and self-discipline in its living groups, because it would be impossible to station a camp teacher all the time in each of these little cabins, and if special emphasis were not put on their self-discipline and cabin pride they would have accidents and discipline problems. He hoped I would have a chance to see how that worked, he said.

"Just exactly what are you trying to do, with this program, for these youngsters in the camps?" I asked him.

He looked hard and intently at me. When Denver Fox wants to, he can turn a piercing gaze in your direction. Then he gave me, quietly and thoughtfully, but obviously from a lifetime of thinking about it, the best statement I have yet heard of the purpose of the camps.

"You know, human beings are so intelligent today," he said, "that they have been able to alter their natural environment to the point where some of us no longer have a natural environment. Some of us live almost entirely in a synthetic environment. It will probably be even more so. Our future is probably a push-button, automated, plastic, concrete, steel world. How can *homo sapiens* relate in a meaningful way to his natural environment? How can he understand natural forces? That is what concerns us up here."

He thought about it a minute.

"What values are we seeking?" he mused. "Above all, we would like to help the child become a more complete person—not only educationally, but spiritually and socially too. To give him experiences he otherwise never would have had. To help him become more self-dependent, more mature, more competent in skills and knowledge. To help him to view the world in new ways of questioning, wondering, discovering, solving problems.

"We try to give every child a chance to have the experience of contributing hard work, very hard work in many instances, toward making this a better land through conservation—planting trees, controlling erosion, reducing the fire hazard—and not just talking about it, but having a chance to get hold of the tools, and use them right, and do a man's work with them.

"We try to give him a chance to meet and understand and make friends with other youngsters from different cultures, different races, different economic levels. We deliberately put him into mixes with some friends, some strangers.

"We try to give him a chance to learn something about responsibility. Even the simple fact that he can take care of himself. He can make his bed. He can sweep his room. He can do these things by himself. He can rely on himself. He can learn a bit more about what democracy means. When he first comes up here, democracy probably means to him the freedom to do this, the freedom to do that. There's one thing that is usually lacking: that is the freedom to be able to accept responsibility for your own actions. One of the real steps in the growth of youngsters comes when they under-stand that responsibility is more than just a word for 'be good.' It really means, 'If I can show I am responsible for this I can continue to enlarge on what I can do as long as I can indicate that I can handle it in a responsible way.' So democracy leads to the acceptance of more responsibility for your activities, and is in that sense a doorway to freedom."

He smiled half apologetically at his own eloquence. "You must have got some sense of this in the orientation today," he said.

"You will probably see here at camp that most of the teaching follows what we sometimes call the *discovery* approach," he said. "I see this as being synonymous with what people think of generally as the 'scientific' approach, or the 'investigative' approach, or the 'problem-solving' approach. One of the sound reasons for using it is that it is just so much more interesting for teachers to teach this way, and for kids to learn. It is a lot more fun when the learner is involved in making discoveries — finding out for himself some new relationships, new insights, new facts, new concepts — and being actively involved in it. This makes learning a great deal of fun. And if we can help youngsters to approach learning through discovering facts and relationships, being alert, questioning, identifying questions and problems, building up the methods of problem solving, then they will have a tool that will help throughout their lives."

He went on. "There's another thing I should add. It is of real value to the classroom teacher who comes up with his students each week to see this problem-solving, discovery approach used with his own students. You've probably noticed that there are five classroom teachers here this week from San Diego and La Mesa with their classes. I think you will hear them say before the week is over that they have gained a great deal from it. Many classroom teachers have said how much it has helped them to be freed for a week of the prime responsibility for teaching their own group, so that they can stand over on the sidelines and see how their youngsters respond to other teaching approaches by other people.

"I think you'll be interested in some of the teaching up here," he said.

I asked Denver whether there were not some special problems involved in being principal of three camp schools 40 miles apart. He said indeed there were, but he manages to be at each of the camps at least once a week, and work closely on problems that crop up.

"One kind of problem you might not think of," he said, "is the rather special need for public relations with the people and groups surrounding mountain camps. If we are going to make use of the out-of-doors we need an outdoors to relate to. Much of our outdoors is on private land, or in a State park, or under the Forest Service. So we have the problem of developing a relationship with the cattlemen, whose whole background has been to keep people off their land to protect their cattle, so that they will let us come

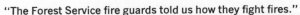

"The Forest Service fire guards told us how they fight fires."

on their land and sometimes do some work on it; with the Forest Service, to help them realize that our sixth graders can actually help, rather than hinder them, with their work; with the State Park, to assure them that we can live in this situation without disturbing the natural museum they have.

"Of course, we always have the problem of stretching the dollar." He smiled. "Fortunately because of the nature of our work we can often make good use of materials turned in by other departments, and therefore we dig through salvage and surplus. So far as our instructional materials are concerned, we can go to the land for much of the material we use. We go down to the desert and pick up a couple of tons of alabaster gypsum. We go out and gather our wood, our bark, our lichen, our plants. We go out and dig up our clay for modeling. This sort of thing makes it rather economical.

"But I have always thought that our task is to have a quality program, rather than just a cheap program," he said. "I think people will pay for quality. This is *not* an inexpensive program. If we had a mediocre program we would have phased out long ago. We know we've got to make the program so good nobody can take it away. I think that's the soundest approach we could make."

We strolled back toward camp, past the Monkey Bridge. This was a structure built from logs stuck into the stream bottom and crossed in X shape. The logs were fastened together in the middle of the X, and a walking rope was stretched along the middle, from the center of one X to the center of the other, with two hand ropes along the top of the X. Pairs of logs were about ten feet apart, and it took eight pairs to span the stream and the swampy little hollow on either side of it. Walking the ropes from X to X required considerable dexterity. The closer we get to the bridge, the louder grew the screams and shouts and laughter. "The Monkey Bridge is one of the high points of the fun at Cuyamaca," said Denver. Every class that comes here tells the next class about it. They'll say, you know that fat fellow from Sunnyside, and they will shake with laughter. They will tell how the poor fellow got halfway between the logs, and got to swinging, and couldn't stop, and pretty soon his feet came off the bottom rope and he was hanging with one hand, and then he dropped off right down in the creek and came up with his pants wet. Every class looks forward to walking the Monkey Bridge. "Of course, you're going to try it, aren't you?" he said with a twinkle.

"Surely," I said, and then thought twice about it, but it was too late because I was caught in a stream of sixth graders and pushed inexorably toward those ropes. Well, it wasn't as bad as I had ex-

The Monkey Bridge — walking the ropes from X to X
required considerable dexterity.

pected. It didn't do any more than sway gently with me. As a matter of fact, I was a minor sensation on the bridge. Because I weighed about a hundred pounds more than the average sixth grader, I created a grand canyon in the bridge whenever I got in the middle between the logs. That in turn created a steep hill on either side of me. And for any 12 year old it is immensely more exciting to go across a bridge made up of hills and valleys than to go over one that is only gently curved. Therefore, I found everyone wanting to go across just before or after me. Little Cindy whose napkin I had sat on at noon seized my hand and cried, "Come on, Bill. Go across again. Make me a hill!" And I might have had a steady job there, but it was the end of the afternoon activity period and there was a general back-to-camp migration in which I was gratefully caught up.

# IV
# MEET A CAMP STAFF

DENVER SAT WITH ME at dinner and helped me place all the camp teachers by name. There seemed to be fifteen of them, if I counted right.

There was Harry, the head counselor, the former track coach, who, Denver said, still liked to run several miles a week, but whose athletic build was now bulging a bit around the middle in tribute to Cuyamaca's good cooking.

There was Walt, the lean, hard ex-woodsman, who still liked to work in the forest service in the summer. Walt, like most of the teachers, was serving as host at a table; Harry was moving around from place to place, taking his food on the run.

Roy and Edna were married, Denver said—the only married couple on the staff. They had been married three years ago, when both were camp teachers, and had decided to stay with outdoor education rather than moving to the city schools. Roy's background was a little like Walt's in that he had worked for the forest service and lumber mills, after graduating from Washington State, and had been assistant head counselor at the two other camps before being transferred to Cuyamaca. Edna was the tall, handsome girl who had been hostess at my table that day at lunch, and had conducted the orientation in Eastwind. Roy was quiet, calm, husky, a person you could tell at first sight was an outdoorsman.

These were the most experienced counselors. Harry had been with the camps for nearly 20 years, Walt for a dozen, Roy for eight, Edna for five. Dottie and Marty had also been with the program for several years. Dottie had graduated from teachers college in New York State with a major in elementary education and an emphasis on science. She worked several years at Palomar, tried teaching in the schools, found she preferred the camps. Marty·was a tall, slim, intense girl who had come from Michigan with a strong background in zoology and a strong prejudice against killing animals. When cold weather drove the field mice inside, Marty handed out cage-traps to catch the mice live, so people would not set spring-traps for them.

There were two pretty girls with a bit of the South in their voices — Isabel, who had graduated from college in Georgia, and was going to teach physical education in San Diego next year; and Jay, whose husband was in the service. As soon as he came back, she too would transfer to the city schools. Another attractive teacher was Carla, who was the musician of the group, and who, I was told, had just gotten engaged to a college student in San Diego.

Four men were among the other staff teachers. Don, a handsome young fellow who had graduated from Santa Barbara and was planning to become an artist and an art teacher. Ernie, the lean leathery fellow who drove the red Porsche to camp and who had once had his own ocean diving service. Augie, a balding young man ( I heard him solemnly telling a group of children that the Indians had scalped him), who had just graduated from teachers training and still commuted 150 miles every Wednesday night to take a course at San Diego State. And Dick, a husky, blonde athletic type who was the only counselor not trained as a teacher. He was employed by the County rather than by the schools; his background was recreation and forestry.

There were also two trainee teachers, completing their college course — Pete, a short, stocky, athletic fellow who was finishing a physical education major at San Diego State; and Jennie, a student at San Diego City College, who was junior enough to be looked after by the older teachers, lithe and slim as a willow and young enough to keep up with the most energetic camper, and pretty and girlish enough to be the darling of the place.

All these were very different personally, and yet there was enough similarity about them to make one think of a "camp teacher type." I thought as I looked around the room at them, that they were an extraordinarily interesting, attractive, well-adjusted, and competent-seeming group, and I asked Denver how he got them. He said they were fortunte in having a number of people wanting to join the camp staffs. He reviews the application folders and then makes a recommendation to the personnel department of the schools.

"What qualities do you look for when you interview a camp teacher applicant?" I asked him.

"In the first place, we try to get a balance," he said. "A balance of science people, recreation, arts and crafts, and so forth. We have to provide a balanced staff in each camp so that we don't end up with a science camp, a recreation camp, and so on. Now, of course, this makes it important that we help them learn the parts of the job they don't know. We can't assume that every new teacher is grounded in every aspect of the program — that a science major knows enough about camping, and a classroom teacher knows enough outdoor education, and vice versa. So we have two and one-half weeks' preliminary inservice education in September, and carry that right on throughout the year with staff discussion, demonstrations, films, making maximum use of our experienced personnel. The meeting on rattlesnakes you saw this morning was a part of our inservice education."

"They don't all have to come with training in outdoor education, then?" I asked.

"We want them to have a sensitivity and a response to the outdoors," he said. "Please don't misunderstand this: I think that *all* teachers in training should have some exposure to and participation in the use of the outdoors as a learning laboratory. This is true whether they go into outdoor education or not; they need it so that they will know how to make a maximum use of the outdoor environment, whether it is on their school grounds, their campus, their canyon, or whatever. But so far as my concern with recruiting teachers goes, I would put formal training of this kind fairly low on the list. I'm more interested in whether they have had courses in the natural sciences, whether they have had good teaching experience, whether they are well-adjusted alert people who like kids, who like other people, who can work closely with others. I want them to have an appreciation and enjoyment of being in the outdoors and being with kids. If they have that I don't worry about whether they have had camping experience.

I asked him whether he didn't have trouble keeping such attractive and lively young people on the staff.

"Indeed we do!" he said. "We have a heavy turnover, and expect it. We try to hire professional teachers, and you find that people who have a basic interest in teaching are willing to try this for a year or two, but ultimately most of them want to get back into the classroom, or to do some more studying and advance themselves in the profession. We have the choice of looking for a professional camper or a top teacher. We could keep the camper longer, but we take the latter choice, even though a teacher may be a short-term investment.

"Also," he said, "you can see that we hire a lot of young teachers. They are at the age to get married. This job takes them away from social life five days a week. When they do get married they don't want to leave home five days a week. So we expect to lose a number of excellent people each year, but are thankful to have had them for even a year or two."

We checked off the people who would probably not be back the next autumn: Isabel, Jay, Augie, the two trainees, two or three others still uncertain. In other words, the turnover was going to be about one half of the present staff.

By this time, dinner was over. The dishwashers and wipers now needed hardly any supervision. The scraps disappeared into Porky and Smokey. The sweepers pushed their brooms energetically around the floor. Denver went to drive a suspected measles case back to San Diego, and I went outside to watch the citizens of Camp Cuyamaca get rid of excess energy.

Most of them were doing this by means of a vigorous play period that intervened between dinner and the evening program. They were throwing and kicking a ball, playing tag, skipping rope, competing in a tug of war. Ernie was in charge, sometimes mopping his brow, enjoying every minute of it.

During the play hour, Isabel was teaching the Weatherbirds the skills they needed to know. The camp had a very good weather station: barometer, wet and dry bulk thermometers, wind indicator, rain gauge, and a device that consisted mainly of short sticks

The counselors led some songs.

to duplicate the amount of moisture in the ground cover. The sticks could be weighed, the amount of moisture calculated, and thus the fire danger estimated. The Weatherbirds had a dittoed sheet on which they filled in the readings twice a day, and, I gathered, then made a weather forecast.

At 7 o'clock, everyone gathered in the Hall of the Winds for a program on "The Story of the Forest." The children were a bit restless, and occasionally a teacher would go over to say a few words to some of them. The folding chairs were rather hard, but even so I was somewhat bemused to see a lad near me systematically taking the seat boards out of his chair until he could sag down in the open framework. Thereafter he seemed quite comfortable.

Isabel and Jay led three songs. Too early in camp, Harry said to me; the campers aren't singing very well yet.

Then Isabel operated the slide projector, while the goodlooking young counselor named Don gave a commentary. The children became absorbed in the color pictures.

They began with San Diego harbor, followed by a long shot back over the coastal plain, and then the mountains. There was a slide of the oak and pine forests around Cuyamaca, and another of the fir and sugar pine forests higher in the mountains. Don told them they would see the high forest when they went on conservation.

Don seemed to be making two points: that the forest is more than just trees; and that the forest is a living community, where many kinds of living things interact within a general framework of natural balance.

He showed them a series of gorgeous color slides of plants— blue lupine on the forest carpet; chaparral, especially the manzanita which he said they would work with in woodcraft; the parasite plants like mistletoe and dodder; and some of the poison plants, like poison oak and nettles. He warned them to be especially careful of the poison oak which at this season would be without leaves and therefore hard to identify. "Everything in the forest contributes something to the community," he said. "Does anyone know what poison oak contributes?"

"Keeps things away?" a boy guessed.

"No," said Don. "It's poisonous to us, but not to many of the birds and animals. It doesn't keep them away; it furnishes berries for them to eat."

Next came a series of slides of the wood birds. Looking at what seemed to be a picture of ordinary mountain foliage, he challenged them to see a bird in it. They oohed and ahed as he showed them twelve baby quail which were really quite invisible until pointed out, so perfectly were they camouflaged by the forest colors. He developed quite skillfully some of the reciprocal relationships in the forest: the tanager eating the berries from plants and then scattering the seeds as it flies so that new plants can spring up elsewhere; the hawk which, by eating some of the small animals keeps the forest from being overrun by the rodents.

Then followed animal slides—rabbit, beaver, fox, woodrat, raccoon, and snakes. The rattlesnake, he said, is the only poisonous snake they have to worry about in this forest. He urged them not to kill snakes just because they are snakes. "The non-poisonous snakes," he said, "are completely harmless to us, and they help maintain the balance of nature in the forest. Every time we kill an animal senselessly, we upset the balance."

He came to a picture of a deer grazing. "Look at that deer," he said. "Eating the plants. He couldn't live without them. On the other hand, he helps nourish the soil so that plants can live. He spreads seeds that become new plants. When he dies, just as when the plants die, he helps to make the soil rich.

"The picture is so lifelike we can imagine the deer is breathing," he said. "And he is, of course. He is breathing out carbon dioxide and breathing in oxygen, just as we are. Now you may not realize that these green plants are breathing, too. The trees and the flowers, every green plant, they all breathe. Why is it, then, the air doesn't become filled with carbon dioxide, and all the oxygen get used up? The secret is the wonderful balancing mechanisms that nature has developed. For instance, these plants take the waste gases out of the air and use them to help manufacture the food they need. And in the process of making their own food they give off a gas which, strangely enough, is the very oxygen we need to breathe."

Isabel flipped the slides. Don talked on quietly. "As you walk through the forest this week, you will have an opportunity to read stories," he said. "Not the kind you find on the magazine stands, but just as interesting. Look at this picture now. What does the story tell you? There has been an animal moving through the snow. Only one set of tracks. Here you can see that the animal was killed. What did it? Probably a bird. See this straight line going into the tracks. Was that where the bird's wing or claws touched as he swooped down? Probably the bird that did this was an owl. At night, or early morning, it swoops down like that with no sound at all. Just a silent swoop. The animal was probably a rabbit. He was probably hurrying to the protection of a bush, because his brown fur would show up too well against the snow. He didn't make it. The owl saw him too early. You might think of this story as a cruel one. But it isn't a question of cruelty. There was no hate in the heart of the bird. He was just eating to survive. Every living thing in the forest must do this.

"What does *this* story tell you?" he asked of another slide. "Here is an animal caught in a trap. This is a story of man's attempt to control nature. Some cattlemen probably found that coyotes were killing their calves. So they set a trap. But man is not all-wise. Instead of catching a coyote, he caught a little fox, which was no threat to the calves and actually was a great friend to man because it killed many of the rodents that cause cattlemen trouble."

The audience attention was very deep at this point.

"Here is another story." The picture on the screen was the burnt out ridge above Camp Cuyamaca. "What do you think happened here?" "Fire," shouted the audience. "Right," said Don. "This was what the great forest fire of 1950 left. Skeletons of trees. Fire is the most terrifying thing in the forest. All the living fear it. After fire comes starvation. Floods. Erosion. Topsoil washes away, and farms are ruined.

"Here is a different kind of story. What do you think was happening in this cut along a new roadbed that someone took a picture of? This is a soil factory. This is what is happening underneath the forest carpet of flowers and grasses. Down here, far below the carpet, are the rocks that put the minerals into the soil. The tree roots dig deep, break up the rocks—see this crack in the rock here? The water seeps into the holes, freezes, crushes the rock, makes new soil. The topsoil here is a living soil. All kinds of plants, animals, insects, worms live in it, making it ready for other plants to live on it."

The picture now was a mountain stream. "Have you ever thought of the forest as a source of water?" he asked. "Much of the water in our country comes from the mountains and the forests. If there hadn't been mountains here, do you think there would ever have been a San Diego or an Oceanside, or a Chula Vista down below?"

"Here is still another story," he said. "You see here a group of campers like you looking at a cave. Is it an animal's cave? Was it a cave used by the Indians for food storage? These campers, like you, will have a chance to look for signs to read that story.

"The Indians didn't hurry through the forest," he said. "They looked carefully as they went. They took time to read the signs around them, and to read stories like these. You do that, up here this week, too. Don't hurry. Look around you. Try to think what is happening. See if you can read the stories in the forest."

I thought it was an extremely good presentation, almost an ideal introduction to a week of school in the mountains, and was a bit surprised to learn that the camp teachers take turns giving the talk. They have a mimeographed outline of the entire lecture prepared for past and future generations of camp teachers. They all vary from it, but the outline makes sure the basic ideas are there.

Don said there could be five minutes for questions. They came very slowly at first, in that large room, and then burst out in a great rush. Don had trouble cutting them off, even after 15 minutes. Strangely enough, it seemed to be the woodrat that was most interesting to them. How long did it take him to build his elaborate house? (Two or three years.) What if it blows over or gets knocked over? (He rebuilds it.) If we tear up his house, would we find some of the things he packs away? (Probably, but it isn't fair to tear up his house.) Whether they got all that Don told them about the balance of nature, and the stories they could read in the forest, I don't know. But they were certainly well informed about the woodrat.

After 15 minutes, the questions were cut off. "Northwind," Ernie called, and his group began to assemble. "Southwind," shouted Pete. "Westwind," called Carla. "Eastwind," said Jay. The four groups went out into the brisk air. It was a good 20 degrees colder than the afternoon had been. I zipped up my golf jacket, and wished that I had brought a winter overcoat.

The staff lounge was warm and the tone was relaxed, as the counselors talked over the first day. I gathered that no unexpected problems had come up on Monday. There seemed to be a certain tension, though, in the way they were looking forward to the rest of the week. I asked about it.

"No sweat," said Walt, the assistant head counselor who had demonstrated the snake kit that morning. "We have a larger group this week, and more behavioral problems among them. Have you seen the list?"

I was surprised to see how much information came from the schools. There were health notes on a number of children: This little girl was a diabetic, and had to take oral insulin every day. This girl was a Christian Scientist, and, therefore, must not have medical care without family permission. This boy had recently had a serious illness and should not take long hikes. This one was allergic to certain foods. This one bleeds easily. This one has enuresis, and should be on a lower bunk. Two children were subject to petit mal, and need daily preventive medication. There was a long list of such things. These would be studied by Carol the nurse, who would arrange for the necessary medicine and indicate activities which certain children should avoid.

There was an even longer set of notes about behavior problems. This information apparently represented the best advice of classroom teachers and principal. Most of the problems were innocuous: Henry is shy. Susan is very shy; try to bring her into groups. Tom lost his mother this winter. Annette daydreams a lot. Linda is very forgetful, and keeps losing things. Another group of notes took this form: A, B, and C act awfully silly when they're together; separate them if you can. D and E aren't good for each other. F and G bring out the worst in each other. H and I are always quarreling. These suggestions had already been taken into account in assigning cabins.

Certain notations were less pleasant. Sam is very withdrawn, tends to be rebellious. Hank is hostile to all kinds of authority. John pouts a lot; lives in a foster home and is quite insecure. Billy is very immature for his age, and is likely to act without thinking. Jimmie has sticky fingers; has been in trouble twice this year for stealing. Two cases stood out: A boy named David had just been re-admitted to school after being suspended for two weeks. This boy won't stand for any kind of authority, they said. The other name that jumped out at me was Dan (or at least we shall call him Dan). The notes on him were long and detailed. He was a real leader, they said, but unfortunately in the wrong sort of thing. He ran with an older group. He had a juvenile hall record for crime. He had caused more trouble this year than any other pupil in school, and they were afraid he was heading toward a bad career. This lad, I recognized, as the sullen handsome boy who I had seen in Northwind and who had sat at the opposite end of my table, talking out of the side of his mouth.

I noticed that a high proportion of these potential "problems" were in Northwind. "Is it going to be pretty rough down there to-night?" I asked.

"Yes, there'll be problems," said Walt. "First night's always a little rough. They aren't used to sleeping with 40 other kids, and they aren't tired enough to go right to sleep. And they haven't got used to the idea of responsibility yet. It's hard to get them quiet. But Ernie can take care of them. He's easygoing, but he's tough."

Ernie was in charge at Northwind.

"What will he do tonight?" I asked.

"Probably offer them a choice between music and a story. Let them run down. Get the lights out by 8:30 or so for the music or the story, if he can. Try to have everything quiet by 9:00. If he can."

"And if they don't quiet."

"Then he'll have to take care of the noisy ones."

Harry had been briefing the classroom teachers who had come along with their students. He had gone over the whole program with them. They would have limited teaching duties and no formal supervisory duties although each of them would be host at a table at meals. Each morning after breakfast they would inspect the four cabins and grade them on cleanliness and orderliness. They would be surprised at how much those scores would mean to the competing cabins, he said. Outside of that they could simply follow along activities, observe their own pupils, and be helpful in any way they could. "Classroom teachers tell us," he said, "that they can often reach a relationship with their students here that they never can in their classrooms. And sometimes you can be of real help to them. One thing to watch out for is homesickness. You may be surprised at some of the children that get homesick up here. We try to encourage them to overcome it. If they do, it's a great victory for them. Some of the childish fright and uncertainty fall away, and they find they have grown up a bit."

A dart game began, and a wild pitch by Jennie cleared out one side of the lounge. That gave me an opportunity to discover one of the hidden advantages of the staff house: The cooks send over a large share of the left-over desserts, along with a supply of milk and fruit. The refrigerator in a pantry off the lounge held two pans of the bread pudding we had been served for lunch, plus a chocolate cake and a gelatine fruit salad from other meals. A coffee pot was bubbling, and I sat down over cake and coffee with a half dozen of the counselors and two classroom teachers who were refugees from the flying darts. One of the San Diego teachers was saying that he was a bit surprised they let David come. "You know what he did?" he said. "He put a dead rat on the platform just before a visiting celebrity came out to speak in assembly. Made him a big hero for a while." We laughed appreciatively.

"Is this group tougher to handle than most of them?" I asked.

"It's too early to tell yet," said Ray in his quiet, half-diffident way. "These kids are lively, and they're not grown up yet, and there are an awful lot of them in a small space. You see we can't take the chance of just letting them wander around, which is what they would probably like to do. Some of them probably resent the supervision, and even the fact that they have scheduled activities up here. And as you know there are some boys in this group who have been in trouble before."

"It'll relax in a day or two," said Isabel.

"Do sixth graders ever get tired?" I asked.

"They go like pistols for a little while," said Roy, "then sit down and rest, and start right up again."

"They're not the distance runner type," said Harry.

"Give them five minutes' rest, and you'd never know they were ever tired," said Isabel.

By this time the mountain air had put me in the uncommon situation of thinking about retiring at 9 p.m. I took a walk with two of the classroom teachers out in the cold night, past the dormitories. A moon had climbed up behind the mesa, and lighted up the sharp edges of ridge and trees — just as though it were an exhibit arranged for us smog-dwellers from the coastal plains who were not used to clear mountain nights. The girls' cabins, as expected, were quieter than the others. No sound at all was coming from the cabin where Jay was in charge; from Carla's cabin, the strains of "Finlandia" drifted softly from a record player. Across the quadrangle, Southwind was sporadically quiet, sporadically noisy with the giggly laughter of adolescent boys and occasionally the instant basso of Pete. Northwind was not quiet at all. There was a buzz of talk, a few hoots and catcalls, an occasional loud laugh. Then came Ernie's lazy drawl, as calm as though he spent every evening in this way. "Look, fellows," he said, "I've let you talk a little longer tonight because it's the first night. How would you like to hear a story now?"

"What about?" called a boy, obviously from one end of the room.

"Hmm," commented one of the visiting teachers.

"I'm glad city schools let out at 2:30," said the other teacher.

I shivered to my room, wrapped tightly in the blankets nurse Carol had found for me ("What are you, a retarded case?" she had asked with a twinkle. "Don't you know you're supposed to bring a bedroll up here?"), and went to sleep at approximately the instant my head touched the cot. I had neglected to bring a pillow, too.

# V
## A HIKE INTO THE FOREST

I AWAKENED ABOUT five minutes later with gray daylight on the floor and people noise in the hallway. Pulling a piece of ice that had been my left foot back into the blankets, I turned over to go back to sleep. Then the full horror of the situation became clear to me: The day at Cuyamaca really *did* begin at 6:30!

At or near 6:30. The longer I was in camp, the more skillful I became in sleeping a little later, defrosting myself, washing, and dressing in a few economical movements, and still appearing in the dining hall with a casual manner intended to suggest that I *always* got to breakfast at 7:00 a.m.

That first morning I put on all the clothes I could find, and debated the idea that I might also wrap up in a blanket. After all, the Indians did. It was a pale day. The sun, if any, was still behind the East Mesa. There was an overcast toward the west, and a few low clouds scudded from west to east before the wind. Up the hill from the quadrangle came four straggling lines — Ernie's army, Carla's tribe, Jay's girls, and Pete's platoon — headed for breakfast, all looking, from a distance, healthy and fit and moun-taineer-like. I filled my lungs with a few gulps of that wonderfully fresh, thin air, and tried to look like a mountaineer, too. But I simply coughed.

Inside the dining room, when the heavy jackets were removed and their occupants could be seen better, a number of sleepy people appeared. I looked particularly at the teachers who had drawn the first night dormitory duty. Pete didn't look especially weary. The others did. Over corn flakes, hot cakes, and sausage, at a table reserved for those who had been on night duty, I tried to inquire tackfully into events of the night. "The girls' cabins," they said, "hadn't been too bad. Southwind hadn't been too bad." "Northwind," said Ernie with his crooked grin, "had been chal-lenging."

"How much sleep did you all get?" I asked. Carla and Jay said they thought they had slept about six hours. Pete, the mesomorph type, said he had got about seven. "It's worse the first night," he said, "How much do you usually get on cabin duty?" I asked. "Eight or nine," he said, filling his plate with hot cakes again. "He's just a growing boy," said Jay.

Ernie said he guessed he might have got four hours' sleep. The kids were awfully slow in quieting down. Finally, had to send two boys named Dan and David out to sit in the shower room for a while so the others could be quiet. "Then I had to wake two boys who were supposed to be bed-wetters, so they could go to the toilet," he said. "A boy got sick and I had to wake up Carol. And about 5 o'clock I woke up again and heard this funny noise. I couldn't figure out what it was. And here were two boys fishing out their suitcases. At five o'clock!"

I had a second cup of coffee and began to feel more like a mountaineer. The eight Weatherbirds came up one by one to the front of the dining hall, told us about their task, and promised a forecast after breakfast. They had a little trouble with "psychrometer," but handled anemometer, barometer, wind vane, rain gauge, moisture sticks, and various kinds of thermometers like veterans. They even described the weather flags, including the blue rectangle on white background which I assumed would be flying that morning to indicate a cold wave. Some of them read their little speeches from a dittoed sheet, but others said it in their own words.

Harry announced that after breakfast the classroom teachers would inspect the quarters and report to the activity meeting, which was scheduled for 9 o'clock, what they found.

By this time I was feeling so much like a mountaineer that I took a walk down to the creek and back past Ill Wind where nurse Carol was finishing morning sick call. Ernie's sick boy had swollen glands, she said; she suspected mumps. Another child had been exposed to measles, and still another to chicken pox, and were showing symptoms. Harry was going to call their parents. Still another boy had a bad sore throat, and she thought he should see a doctor. Outside of that, just the usual run of camp troubles.

A poised little girl came in while I was talking to Carol. She had a long splinter in her foot.

"You're all right," said the nurse.

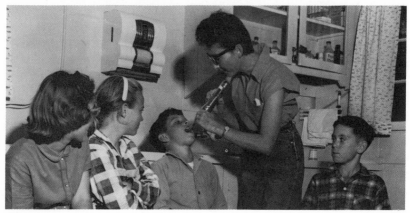

"Doctor, you think we should operate?" Carol asked me.

"Do you ever shoot people with troubles like this?" I asked. "It seems to me they shoot horses that have troubles with their feet."

"Ohhh," gasped the girl. Then her face relaxed in a wonderfully relieved smile. "You're kidding," she said.

Carol took care of the splinter quickly and efficiently with an antiseptic, tweezers, and band-aid.

A thin little boy with a short green sweatshirt and a longbilled yellow cap was watching the scene from across the room, where he had been having his temperature checked.

"You're all right," said Carol, when she took the thermometer out of his mouth, "Just a little excited last night, I guess. What activity are you going on this morning?"

"Don't know," said the boy. "Doc, you going on an activity?" So I became Doc.

"I think I'll go on one of the field hikes," I said.

"Think I'll go on one too," he said.

"What's your name?" I asked him.

"George," he said, "See you later, Doc," he tossed over his shoulder as he galloped toward Northwind.

At 8:45, the sun had finally climbed the mesa, and was looking tentatively down on four thin lines of campers, drawn up in a hollow square in the inner quadrangle. Four camp teachers tried to shape them up into something like a military appearance. I found a place where the sun fell comfortingly on the back of my neck. A small girl hit a gong, two other girls pulled the rope that raised the stars and stripes and the California bear to the top of a flagpole, and everybody recited the pledge to the flag and sang "God Bless America." It wasn't exactly as impressive as the changing of the guard at Buckingham Palace, but it got the day started. Everybody moved into the Hall of the Winds for the morning "activity meeting."

Here we got the weather news. Yesterday's high was 60, last night's low was 36. It just seemed colder. I didn't catch the wind reading or the relative humidity, but the forest fire danger (figured from the moisture in the fuel sticks) was medium high, and the forecast was "fair."

One of the classroom teachers from San Diego came up to report on their cabin inspection.

Northwind, he suggested mildly, left something to be desired. Shoes were on top of some bunks. There was a bar of soap on the floor — what if you would step on it and break a bone! There was trash in the drains. Score: 8.6 out of 10. Some of the Northwind

"Everybody in the pledge to the flag . . ."

boys looked rather pleased; they had expected worse. The teacher explained that they graded leniently this morning because Harry had served them the "milk of human kindness" with the hot cakes. But tomorrow . . .

Southwind, on the other hand, was better. The floors were wet in both rooms, and suitcases were not lined up under the bunks. That was all they could find wrong. Score: 9.7 out of 10. The Southwind boys looked rather superior.

In Westwind, they had found only a gum wrapper in the shower (where there's a wrapper, there must be gum), a dirty mirror, and some dust behind one of the heaters. If they had looked behind the radiators in the boy's cabins, as they were going to do tomorrow, he said . . . Score: 9.9 out of 10. Carla looked pleased.

In Eastwind they couldn't find anything wrong at all. Things were spotless. Score: 10 out of 10. Eastwind was the first day's winner. Some applause from the girls. Jay beamed over her little group.

Harry said that the scores were very close, and that a good performance the next day would put even the lowest cabin back into the running. Then he read lists of names for the morning activities, which seemed mostly to be hikes directed to the study of forest trees, field science, rocks and minerals, forest products, Indian lore and geology, and wildlife and tracking. There was also conservation. I decided to postpone conservation for a day or so, and trooped along with the group who were gathering around

Roy and Jennie. I was glad I did, because it turned out to be a general introduction to the forest environment.

There were 21 of us, altogether. George with his yellow cap. Marie with the Spanish eyes and complexion. The little fellow with the New York Yankees jacket. John, the gangling, withdrawn boy who lived with his "aunt." One or two of the others said "Hello, Bill," or "Hello, Doc" to me, but most of the hikers I didn't know by name. Someone said cheerily, "Where does somebody go to get his money refunded?" and I recognized the boy with the red turtle-neck. He had replaced it with a quilted jacket. George said, "Hi, Doc," and fell into line behind me. "You know, you're about as big as my dad," he said.

We rode a mile or two, apparently to plug into the hike midway, and climbed off where a forest road left the paved highway. Roy gathered his little group, and discussed with them some of the requirements of hiking safely. Much more quickly, and somewhat less permissively than at the orientation session, a set of rules emerged. What might the problems be? Getting lost. Poison oak. Rattlesnakes. Tearing your clothes. Spraining an ankle. How to avoid such troubles? Don't stray from the group. When we're moving, stay behind the teacher; he is experienced in the woods, and will pick a safe path. Don't put your hands under rocks or logs. If you see a snake, what do you do? You don't pick it up. You don't run; the snake might misinterpret a quick action. You don't hit at it; you might miss, and, anyway, if it isn't poisonous, you don't want to kill it. The custom worked out by many generations of campers, said Roy, is to stand still, and yell "freeze!" Then everybody freezes, until the teacher has a good look at the snake and decides whether it is poisonous. "Is that what your stick is for?" a boy asked. "Yes, if we have to, we can hit a snake with it or pin him down," said Roy.

Roy told them to look over at a row of low plants and see if they could tell him which was poison oak. They couldn't, and he said it was hard to see in this season when the leaves weren't out. He pointed out the plant to them and told them to remember its shape and the way the twigs came out.

"And watch out for the chaparral," said Jennie. "It's more dangerous than it looks. It catches you. It catches your belt or your hair. If you squeeze through it, sometimes you can't get back because the branches are pointed wrong for you. It's like fighting a riptide in the ocean."

Roy told them a story that Walt tells about a time when he was crawling through the chaparral on West Mesa and found himself looking right into the face of a rattler. He couldn't back up and the snake didn't want to. "If Walt hadn't looked so mean at the snake, it might have been a bad situation. But old Walt says he looked right firmly at that snake, and it backed up and disappeared."

He thought about that a minute. "You know," he said with a chuckle, "I don't think I'd try that, if I were you. I don't believe you can look as mean as Walt!

Away to the woods!

"Let's go," he said, and swung away into the woods. He carried his snake stick, and looked right and left. We strung out behind in single file. Jennie, with her stick and first aid kit, was rear guard.

I had forgotten how much fun it was to hike in mountain air. Now I stretched out my leg muscles and breathed down to my diaphragm, and felt healthy and young and vigorous and ready to climb Everest if anyone asked me to. At least I felt so until the first rest stop. I had noticed that the teachers apparently tried to fit the pace to the slowest member of the group, and stopped often enough for observations and questions to keep the members from tiring. But at the first stop I had a moment when I wondered whether perhaps I was the anchor on the party. We had been steaming up a grade. I was breathing deeply and trying not to pant, and hoping that the climb was not too steep for the smaller boys and girls. But when I collapsed gratefully on a rock, one of the small boys, instead of collapsing beside me, walked ten feet farther *on his hands!* That was deflation number one. The second one came when I heard two boys talking behind me. Gray sweater: "Why do we have to stop so often?" Black sweater: "Oh, we can't go too fast for the old folks and the girls."

Somewhat chastened, I got back into line, stuck out my chest, pulled in my stomach, and creaked in my ancient way up a stream bed amidst gorgeous stands of pine and oak. They pointed out this kind of tree and that kind of bush, and identified poison oak. We came out in a meadow, and Roy asked, "What's all this around us?"

"Chaparral," the children shouted. What kind of chaparral? They decided it was manzanita, and picked out the telltale signs by which manzanita could be identified.

"I wonder why some mountain slopes are covered with chaparral, and some with tall trees?" Roy mused.

There was discussion. Trees grow where it's higher? Where it's lower, too, a girl said, pointing to a slope below them. Where there's more water? Roy worked the discussion around to the idea that one of them might take better soil. Which one? The children decided the pines needed better soil.

"If I would dig up this chaparral for you, you would see that the roots are nearly twice as deep as the bush is high," said Roy. "They dig down that far to get water. That's why the chaparral lives in poorer soil."

He paused a moment. "At least, that's what *I* say. Now, how could you test that without digging up one of these bushes?"

They thought about that a little while, and a tall boy in a red jacket suggested that they might find a place where a bank was undercut and look at the roots. And sure enough, not far away was an undercut, and we could see that the roots of the chaparral were indeed very long.

I came to expect this kind of field experience, in which the children learned to solve natural problems they observed around them. They were becoming more alert. A girl asked what were some black spots on a tree about ten feet above the ground. "What might have caused them?" Roy asked. Woodpeckers? They compared them with some holes that had indubitably been made by woodpeckers, and there seemed to be little resemblance. Had they been made by another tree falling and striking this tree? Maybe the sap came out and covered the wound, a boy suggested.

Roy said that was very plausible. The marks were too far up to be examined closely, he said. How could they get a better look at them? Climb the tree? No, they weren't climbing trees this week. Field glasses? Yes, but no one has a pair today. Perhaps they could look for similar marks a little lower on a tree. And that is what they did.

We began to sort out the ways of telling one tree from another. The ponderosa pine had a yellowish tint. The Jeffrey pine had a sweet smell. "Like butterscotch," said Maria. A little later, they were all sniffing at a grove, and proudly picking out a Jeffrey pine. They learned what was a Kellogg black oak, and a boy asked whether it was called that because its leaves crackled like corn flakes when you stepped on them. "If we can find some, let's try it," said Roy.

This is what was going on all the time. It was about as different from lecture teaching as it could be. The teacher was telling them comparatively little, but was priming them with questions, and urging them to look for evidence, and think a problem out.

There was a slight sensation toward the rear of our line. John was casually heaving rocks into the underbrush. Jennie spoke to him, and he stopped throwing, but hung back, head down and eyes averted. She stayed back with him a while, then moved up with the rest of the hikers. John lagged farther behind.

When we stopped to look at some different kinds of grasses, and a hole that might have been a coyote's den, Roy had a quiet word with Jennie. "What's wrong with him, back there?" he asked. "I stopped him throwing rocks," she said. "Afraid he's pouting."

When we started up again, Roy went back to John. "I want you to walk up here with me now," he said. John came almost gratefully, and for the rest of the hike stayed with Roy.

About this time, the Yankee boy developed a headache. George gave him his yellow cap. "Maybe it's the light," he suggested. "How about a drink of water?" asked Jennie. She poured it into his mouth from six inches above. Camp style. So the mouth didn't touch the canteen.

"What's this?" said Roy suddenly, and bent over some tracks. We decided they were almost certainly deer. Was it running or walking? They talked about that. "How could you tell?" asked Roy. "How would the tracks look different?" They'd be deeper, it was suggested. Why? Because you come down heavier; you're farther up in the air and coming down hard. When you run, are your footprints going to be farther apart or closer? "Let's test it out," suggested Roy. "Here's some sandy ground that's not muddy and still ought to leave prints. Carol, you run across it, and Linda, you walk. Then let's look at the tracks."

"They're farther apart when you run," said George. They noted that there is a deep place in the footprint when you run. Why? Because you have to push off — like jumping. So the deer was walking. The tracks were shallow and flat, and rather close together. "Was the deer frightened?" Roy asked. Apparently not, they decided; just walking through a muddy place.

We sat down at the edge of a glade—like "a room in the woods," Jennie said — and tried to keep quiet and listen to the forest.

"I can hear a tree creaking," said a girl.

"I can hear my stomach growling," a boy said sotto voce.

"Shut up!" said the boy beside him.

"Let's be quiet and listen to the woods," said Roy.

We kept quiet and let the sound of the woods come to us. It was a fine moment. The sounds around us were things I hadn't listened to for a long time. Or perhaps they had just been hidden under the thrumming and pulsing sounds of the city. The first

"Was the deer running or walking?"

sounds I recognized were leaf and branch sounds, and then the wind itself sighing — a sound I had been completely unaware of as we walked. We watched the wind make a wave that moved across the open meadow toward us, and passed with a gentle rustle. I found I could separate out four or five different bird voices, and the high-pitched irritated chatter of a chipmunk. From a great distance came a baritone call that might have been a cow or a mountain lion or almost any other large animal. There was a faint drip-drip-drip of water, perhaps a spring. I became conscious of little rustles and movements near me, which might have been wind or the signs of insects and lizards yet unseen.

And at that moment — just as though the scene were staged — a deer moved out of the woods not 200 feet in front of us. Its head was high, and its nostrils twitched. Then it exploded in a flash of brown and white across the meadow and into the forest on the other side.

"What kind of deer was it?" asked Roy, when the buzz of excitement had subsided.

"A doe?"

"How could you tell?"

"No antlers?"

"Does a deer ever lose its antlers?"

They talked about that, and why a deer rubbed against trees, and then Roy asked what family of deer it was.

"A mule deer," said a boy. It was Money-back.

"Good," said Roy. How can you tell it's a mule deer?"

"Antlers?" said somebody.

They laughed him down.

"Big ears?"

"Tail?"

Roy said the tail was the best way to tell them, but they did have big ears. Then we went to try to find the prints of the animal that had performed for us, and check whether the tracks of a running deer really looked as we had said they would.

That's the way it went. We talked about signs of an old forest fire we saw on a distant ridge, some signs of erosion, a rock or two, and some mistletoe which led into a discussion of parasites. With the nice way he had of relieving the tension of learning, Roy pointed out a magnificent yucca, seven feet tall, and in full bloom, and suggested we sit down and enjoy it a few minutes.

I sat down and enjoyed it thoroughly. But the sixth graders were able to sit down for approximately 90 seconds. Then they were up, dashing around, identifying something, going to Roy for confirmation, pulling out small cameras, taking pictures of the yucca, the woods, even of Roy and Jennie and me. George took a picture of me. 'You're about as big as my dad," he said.

"What does your dad do?" I asked.

"He's in Vietnam," the boy said.

"Has he been there a long time?"

"A year."

"Is he a Marine?"

George hesitated. "He drives a machine," he said finally.

When we started down the mountain again, George put his small hand in mine, and we walked along together.

Roy pointed out some lichen on a rock. "Can any of you guess why this is called pioneer plant?" he asked. The boy with the red jacket, who seemed to know a lot about rocks, figured that one out. It was pioneering new ground. It was breaking up the rock to make soil, so trees and grass could live in it.

By this time it was a pretty fine day. The sun shone about half the time, the grass was relatively dry, the wind not too cold, the woods fragrant.

We came to another opening in the woods where obviously many visitors had stopped on other days. There was no underbrush, the grass was flattened, and there was a carpet of acorns on the ground.

"Look around here a little," suggested Roy.

In a few seconds there was an exclamation of surprise from a girl. She brought Jennie a brown fragment. "Looks like a piece of bowl," she said.

"It is," said Jennie. "Do you suppose somebody's been having a picnic, or is there some other reason for that being here?"

By his time they were finding pottery chunks all over, and a boy had identified a stone that looked as though it might have been used for grinding. "It's an Indian village," a boy announced with conviction. They were more excited than I had seen them before. They scuffed around the acorns, turning up a piece of pottery here, a shaped stone there.

"How can you be sure it was an Indian village?" asked Roy.

"Pots?"

"Anything else? Look how black this soil is. Why would it be so black?"

There were some miscellaneous answers, none of them very close to the target.

"What would the Indians have done here that might have turned the soil black?"

"I don't know," said Money-back.

"If they had a cooking fire, wouldn't it turn the soil black?"

"Could this be an Indian storage cave?"

"That's for sure," said the boy with the black sweater.

"And if they had a fire every day for a long time it would probably leave the ground black for a long time."

They agreed it would.

"Where do you think the dwellings were?"

They became city planners for a few minutes.

"There must have been a teepee right here."

"Wait a minute," said Jennie. "Did these California Indians live in teepees?"

"No, it was a kind of house." The girl who said this was wearing a San Diego College sweatshirt.

"They called it a wickiup," said Jennie. "It was made out of brush and grass and willow branches. There's one back in the Indian building at camp. Didn't you see it?"

"They were sure busy grinding acorns," said George.

What did they live on, besides meat?" asked Jennie.

"Berries."

"Nuts."

"That's why they were so busy grinding acorns, then."

"Can we take home some pottery?" asked one of the girls.

"No, let's leave it for others to see," said Roy. "Maybe you can find some arrowheads. If there was erosion from the rain it ought to turn up some arrow points."

"I've got one," said a boy triumphantly. "Isn't this one?"

"Look at it closely. What do you think?" said Roy.

"Too big, I think."

"Doesn't look as though it was made purposely."

"How did they make arrows?" a boy asked.

Roy talked that over briefly with them, and said that they could try it themselves, if they wanted to, when they got back to camp.

"Can't I take this one home?" Yankee pleaded.

"No, this State Park rule is an important one," said Roy. "If it weren't for such rules these bits of pottery would have disappeared long ago, and we wouldn't be able to see any now."

"Watch out for the cactus," Jennie warned the little cluster of boys studying the arrow point. "They're sharp as a needle."

"I know," said Money-back ruefully, pulling out a needle of prickly pear.

After the village everything was downhill, literally and figuratively.

We sang as we walked,

I like the forest, I love the chaparral,
I like the mountains, I love the rolling hills,
I like a fireside when the lights are low,
    Boom de yah dah, boom de yah dah,
    Boom de yah dah, boom!

It wasn't much of a chorus, but it was fine to keep step to.

We sang,

I'm happy when I'm hiking,
Pack upon my back . . .
    Tramp, tramp, tramp!

Then they found the lizard. Roy held him, but John was beaming proudly. "I saw him first," he said. "I found him." No more pouting. The little lizard looked exactly like an alligator, except that he was green, and only eight inches long. Roy held him behind the head and put a twig in his mouth to show how sharp his teeth were. There was considerable discussion over whether to dissect him for biology, but Roy put some questions that raised a compassionate response, and it was finally decided to let him live. When we came down the last slopes, over the stream, and into camp again, it was time to wash up for lunch.

The other field groups were back by this time, too. One of them had found footprints of half a dozen animals and put plaster in the prints so they could pick up the casts in the afternoon. Still another group had seen three deer and a woodrat's house. Another came back talking about "ecology," which must not have been a familiar word to most of them before that day. And when Marty's group came back, she took David right away to Ill Wind. "He picked up this lizard although we told him not to," she said, "and it bit a finger on his left hand. Then he went back and picked it up again, and it bit a finger on his right hand."

"Do you think he ought to have rabies injections?" someone asked.

"Do lizards have rabies?" asked the nurse. "This might be a medical first."

She decided to find out whether David's parents wanted him to have a tetanus shot. They did.

Pete suggested privately that maybe they should give the lizard a shot, too. "He might be in more danger than the boy. Would *you* want to bite David?"

"Well," said Ernie, "there was one time last night, when we were trying to get Northwind to quiet down . . ."

# VI
## RELATING TO MAN'S ENVIRONMENT

TUESDAY NOON I noticed a change in the tone of the camp. For one thing it was possible to have a conversation at lunch; Monday noon, it had been practically impossible. The children seemed quieter, more relaxed. They seemed to feel less need to test out the teachers to see how far they could go; that was now pretty well known; and as a matter of fact, after the teachers insisted that the children themselves take so much of the responsibility for rule-making it became less challenging to break a rule or put something over on a teacher. There were now fewer unknowns about the camp; the routine had taken over. And there was the combination of cold air and exercise. Most of the sixth graders had taken a long hike Tuesday morning. After lunch, they settled almost grate-fully into a quiet hour.

I noticed that Harry spent much of the lunch hour talking to a little girl whom I judged to be one of his homesick cases, and who seemed not to be touching her food. At the end of the meal, he went over and said a few words to Dan, the sullen looking boy whose teachers had warned the camp about him. He took Dan somewhere with him.

The boys at my table exchanged glances full of meaning.

"What's happened?" I asked.

"Ah, he called one of the teachers stupid and said he'd be damned if he kept in line on her hike," said a boy from La Mesa. Apparently the grapevine was good enough to circulate this news even before lunch.

"What do you think Harry ought to do?" I asked them.

They shrugged shoulders; no one cared to answer.

On my way from lunch, I saw Dan sitting in Harry's office, writing. From the stormy glances he was turning on the page, I judged it was no love letter.

That afternoon I table-hopped among the craft groups. Most of them had moved outside to the unpainted tables. Other groups left doors and windows open, because the sun was now shining at intervals through the hazy clouds and the air was warmer and carried odors of pine oil and drying grass.

I began with the rock craft group, where Don and Edna were in charge. The boys and girls leaned against heavy tables in the hut, and Dave introduced them to the art of shaping rocks.

"If we are going to try to be craftsmen," he said, "What is the first thing we need to do?"

"Wash our hands?" ventured a little girl with a piping voice.

"Know how to use tools?" suggested a tall boy.

Don thought about that a moment. "Yes," he said, "but something else even more important. Anybody have a suggestion? Well, before we start, don't we have to have an idea what we are going to make?"

Heads nodded. Don warmed up to this idea. Obviously, he enjoyed talking about the artist's role. He was surrounded by stone trays, pencil holders, candle holders, and other articles made by previous classes or perhaps by the counselors themselves. Here are some things other people have made, he explained; but you probably have your own ideas what you want to make. You ought to have an idea what you are going to make before you select a rock to work on. Now, how do you select a rock, he asked.

"How can we use this tool safely?"

They decided it made a difference what color and shape it was. "Anything else?" Dave asked.

John came up with the idea that it made a difference how hard the rock was. He was recovered from his morning pout, and indeed had acted like a different boy ever since he had found the lizard. "Very good!" said Don, and showed them a picture chart of rocks ordered by hardness from soapstone, somewhere near the bottom, to diamond at the top. For most of these he had samples, and the children handed the rocks around and compared them with the pictures.

Then Don introduced them to the tools they could use. "What's the most important word for us to remember now?" "Safety!" half a dozen said at once. The idea was getting over.

Don showed them how to use saws, files, drills, and a polishing wheel. They selected rocks from well-stocked bins, and started happily to work.

"What are you making?" I asked John, as he bent his angular frame almost double and sighted along the edge of a piece of soapstone. "Pencil holder," he said. Maria was making a candlestick. A mischievous big fellow with very red windburned cheeks was filing a piece of rock that was beginning to look a little like a cube. "What's it going to be?" I asked. "A pair of dice," he said with a grin. Neither Don nor Edna seemed at all taken aback by that artistic goal.

One of the girls had filed a piece of alabaster gypsum down to a fairly smooth surface. Edna showed her how to smooth it further with coarse and then fine sandpaper, and put a few drops of water on it to bring out the colors. The rock had been a milky white; now areas of rose and gold stood out. The children gathered around to admire. Don explained it was sedimentary work, and the different minerals were deposited by the water and pressed together.

I went over to the tables where a group was working on miniature gardens. These are arrangements of pieces of twig, pine needles, cones, rock, bark, and so forth, that please the craftsman, and often look somewhat like an oriental garden. They make attractive little table pieces, and are perhaps the most nearly

Making miniature gardens — "beauty in natural things."

Clay is more fun when you dig it up and grind it yourself.

finished looking of all the crafts products from Cuyamaca. Samples of miniature gardens from previous classes were all around. They looked like trees and bushes, and some had little men, boats, and garden houses in them.

Components for the gardens were in low boxes. The children tried different combinations to see which pleased them. Dottie went from child to child, making a suggestion here, answering a question there, occasionally holding up an especially interesting product for all to see. No, you won't have to drill a hole for that, she said. Why don't you take a twig with a lot of needles on it? That's very nice, but you might want to fasten it down a little tighter. And so on around the circle. The boys and girls were completely absorbed in what they were doing. I doubt that they even saw me.

At another set of tables, Marty and Dick were supervising the workers in clay. They had dug their own clay — feldspar deposits from the creek banks, streaked with red lines of iron — and were making what I in my youth would have called mud pies. They shaped these pies of clay and water and let them dry. The camp had neither potter's wheel nor kiln, but the mud was beginning to look like ash trays and saucers. Thin sunlight was breaking through the overcast and falling on the backs of the children's necks as they bent over their work, but the breeze was sharp down the camp street.

In the wood shop, Jay was presiding, no longer showing any effects of losing sleep the night before. The children were scraping and cleaning out the burls. It was the same kind of experience as wetting the smoothed alabaster gypsum, for the gray manzanita turned a lovely creamy white, the burls a rich red brown. Like other ignorant visitors I had no idea that the scrubby chaparral hid beauty like that. The children seemed to be making candelabras, if they were making anything. For the most part, they were simply enjoying the metamorphosis of the wood into a thing of beauty, admiring its color and shape. What they produced they would probably take home as a wall piece or just a souvenir.

Carla was in the biology room, supervising Indian crafts. Here the modal behavior was making necklaces of acorns. Some children were shaping stone amulets and drilling them to fit on strings. One boy was learning how to flake arrowheads in the old Indian way, with a pad of leather on his hand, pushing against a piece of hard stone with a piece of bone, shaping the arrowhead one flake at a time. He finally achieved something that looked pointed, and everybody exclaimed in admiration.

At nearby tables, Isabel and Pete had a little group absorbed in molds of animal tracks. On the morning hike they had left plaster to dry in deer and raccoon tracks and something else that they thought might be the track of a coyote. Some of the molds hadn't come out very well because the ground had been too dry and had crumbled under the plaster. But still the molds showed the essentials of the footprint, and Isabel was leading a long discussion on how different animals walk and what you can tell about them from their footprints. Why are a dog's claws out and a cat's claws sheathed when they walk? (To keep claws sharp for tree climbing, and tearing.) How does a footprint look different when an animal is running? (Well, think of how your foot works when you run, and when you walk.) How can you tell when a track is fresh? (Sharp edges.) Now look at this track; what would an Indian boy or girl have known about the animal that produced it? (Fourteen young residents of modern California bent over the table, trying perhaps for the first time in their lives to think and feel as the old residents of California must have thought and felt.)

I went past the rock workers again. The mischievous boy had given up his project of making dice. Couldn't get them flat, he said. But he was turning out a very respectable pencil holder from what was intended to be a six-faced cube. In the Indian group, several campers were modeling their necklaces. In the wood room, the manzanita was becoming more and more beautiful with work, and the children were asking whether they could take their wood home and work more on it. Surely, said Jay; it comes from outside the Park.

It was a full afternoon. The campers washed the crafts off their hands, had a huge turkey chow mein with salad and apple pie, and came back to the dining hall, after the play hour, for an Indian ceremony.

I saw some of the preparations for this ceremony. Walt, Ernie, and Jennie were to be the Indians that evening. "Jennie is everybody's Indian," Harry had explained to me, and Pete said appreciatively, "Jennie heap fine squaw!" She had enclosed her slim lithe figure in a brown squaw dress, a single feather on her head, and looked as though she wanted to break into an Indian dance at any second.

Ernie topped his costume with a gorgeous feather bonnet that reached almost to his heels. It was a plains Indian headdress, he said; the California Indians didn't usually wear anything that gorgeous. "Will anybody notice if I wear argyle socks?" he asked Walt.

Walt seemed to be the most concerned of the three actors. This was apparently because he had to make the fire. He put on his costume, and then spent a long time assembling the materials for fire making. These were an alder wood spindle about eight inches long, an alder board with a shallow hole for the head of the spindle, a fire pan heaped with shredded cedar bark to retain the sparks that would supposedly come from the spindle, and a manzanita bow strung with a thong of deer hide. When he put the spindle in the base board, wrapped the deer thong around it, and pulled the bow rapidly back and forth, a small cloud of smoke and a campfire smell arose.

"Trouble is," Walt said, "you can't ever tell how easy it's going to be to make fire this way. With a little moisture in the air, you just don't produce big enough sparks. So I'm practicing a little."

"No Prometheus he," chuckled Harry.

"If I were doing it, I'd put a few match heads in that mixture," said Henry.

They held this ceremony outside whenever possible, and used the sparks to light a campfire. But the Weatherbirds had turned in a rather tentative forecast that evening (might be fair, because the barometer was still holding steady, but on the other hand — ), and to the rest of us the evening seemed pretty cold and damp. Harry decreed that the Indian ceremony would be held in the dining hall in front of the big fireplace.

The room was nearly dark. Half a dozen candles lighted the space around the fireplace. Tables were pushed back and the children seated on the floor. They were attentive and expectant—quite a difference from Monday night. Harry set the stage with a little talk about the ceremony they were to see.

We don't know when the first Council Ring was held, he said. From the beginning of time men have sat around the fire, singing, dancing, telling stories, performing religious ceremonies. The Council Ring has always been consecrated to the brotherhood of man and the mystery of the Creator.

From outside we heard a chant, in monosyllables which I assumed to be Indian. The three Indians entered — Jennie, the slim squaw beating a flat drum; Ernie, with his long chief's bonnet; Walt, the fire maker, with his bag of materials. Three pretty impressive Indians, lean and tanned and solemn.

Ernie, flanked by the squaw and the fire maker, told the legend of fire. In the beginning, he said, there were no fires except those that came up from volcanoes and down from the skies. But there was one tribe that had a very wise chief, and he saw the need of his people. One day he left the tribe and went into the forest to seek a sign from Wakonda, the Great Spirit. He had a vision or dream of a great storm. So violent was the storm that giant trees were uprooted and thrown about. One such tree was thrown against another, and the force of the wind caused the two trees to rub together. Smoke came from where the trees were rubbing, and then fire. But rain came with the storm, and put out the fire. The chief wakened and gave thanks to Wakonda for the sign.

The wise chief returned to his people, told them about the sign from the Great Spirit, then went around picking up different kinds and pieces of wood to discover which had the spark of fire. After much practice he discovered the secret, and ever after that his people have had fire.

"Fire Maker!" Ernie called. "Bring forth fire."

Walt opened his sack and began to assemble the materials with which he had been practicing. He put them in a little pile. He put his hands on his chest and then lifted his arms toward the sky.

Ernie said, "To Wakonda, the one Great Spirit, that His Wisdom be with us."

Walt extended his arms toward the ground.

"To Mahkah EEnah, Mother Earth, that she send us food," said Ernie.

The Fire Maker then turned to each of the four winds:

"To Wee-yo-pee-atah, the Sunset Wind, that he come not with his strength upon us.

"To Wahzee-yahtah, the Winter Wind, that he harms us not with his cold.

"To Wee-yo-hinyan-pahtah, the Sunrise Wind, that he trouble us not with his hot, dry heat.

"To O-kah-gah, the Rain Wind, that he strike us not with his fierce storms."

At the moment I could have used a little Wee-yo-hinyan-pahtah. The room was chill, but the boys and girls, seated close together, seemed not to be bothered by the temperature. I slid over closer to Isabel, and improved both the temperature and the aesthetics of the situation.

Walt bowed his head a minute, and then began to make the fire. He arranged the base board, the fire pan, the shredded bark, the spindle. He carefully wrapped the thong around the spindle. He positioned the bow, and looked searchingly over his handiwork. He pulled the bow vigorously back and forth. Smoke. Campfire odor. The children exclaimed in surprise. Walt stopped. So far as I could see, there were no sparks.

Walt pulled his bow again. Smoke. Smell. No fire.

A third time. An impressive cloud of smoke. No fire.

"He sometimes has a time trying to make the thing catch," whispered Henry.

Walt reached back into his sack, got out another fire board and spindle, and installed them in the system. He pulled the bow back and forth again. Smoke, odor, no fire. He stopped and rested. Tried again.

He looked at Ernie. Ernie took one end of the bow, and they made it fly back and forth, while the spindle spun and smoked. No fire. They rested a moment, then pulled together. Again. And again. And again. They stopped to rest.

"Need real Indian," whispered Isabel.

"Need real match," whispered Augie.

The children were quiet and concerned, not amused or scornful. There was no laughter, and only a few whispers. You could see shoulders almost visibly straining in empathy with the two Indians who wearily pulled the bow back and forth. Quantities of black smoke rose from the hot spindle.

Then there were sparks. Walt arose with the handful of shredded bark in the fire pan. He blew on it, to fan the sparks. The pan glowed, and then flamed. Walt threw the contents into the fireplace, where a very modern fire had been laid with plenty of flammable kindling, and the whole room danced with firelight.

Subdued expressions of delight from the children.

Only Roy seemed depressed. "I've got to make the fire next week," he explained.

While the firelight danced over the hall and warmed us, the three Indians continued the ceremony. Jennie told a story in sign language, while Ernie interpreted in redskin English. Jennie explained the symbolism of Ernie's bonnet. Jennie danced. She won my nomination for "everybody's Indian," too. During this time, Walt was resting from his labors. Then Jennie beat the drum while Walt did the Eagle dance in the firelight around a stump. At the end of the dance, he leaped off the stump toward the audience, with a shout. The nearby children shrieked.

Ernie swirled his bonnet around to the proper side, and made a final thematic speech. Rather moralistic in tone. Something like this: Even as the flame of the fire joins us together as a single group drawing warmth and comfort together, so may the flame of friendship and good fellowship draw us nearer throughout this week, and may we feel the spark of consideration and understanding burst into full flame (but more quickly! I added silently) and comfort us with increased enjoyment and appreciation of all that is to be had here in this beautiful land of adventure and exploration.

I don't see how he could have said exactly that, but that is what I found written in my notes. In any case, the Indians danced out to the beat of Jennie's drum, and the rest of us got up on our stiff legs and went Indian file to our various cabins.

I passed Harry on my way to the staff house, and asked him what he had Dan writing in his office, early in the afternoon.

"We had a little insubordination," he said. "With this boy, you can't let it pass. I gave him a pad, and told him he had exactly an hour to write down some good arguments why we should not send him home. I said I was going to be hard to convince. He sat there and chewed his pencil and crossed lines out, and at the end of an hour came and asked me for a little longer.

"I honestly expected he would choose to go home. But you know, he doesn't want to go, even though he doesn't want to show us he likes it here. He's willing to write half the afternoon to stay.

"It's almost as though he wants to be punished," mused Harry. "I think if we had ignored this one, he would have been a little disappointed. Strange."

"And gone on to do something worse?" I asked.

"Perhaps. We'll limit his program of activities and see what he does now."

In the staff lounge, I had a few minutes to talk with Roy and Edna.

"I expected to find you assigned to the dormitories tonight," I said.

"Tomorrow," Edna explained.

I asked whether it were true that the assignment of "sleeping in" with the children in their cabins was the one the teachers most dislike. They said this was true. "The more experienced they are, the more they dislike it," said Roy. "You see, you are on duty from the time they go to bed until they get up in the morning. If anything happens, it's necessary for you to be there to take care of it."

"How many hours do you work a week?" I asked.

"There was a time-study on the Palomar schedule once," Roy said, "and the time on duty of some of the teachers between 9:30 Monday morning and 1 or 2 o'clock Friday afternoon ran as high as 67½ hours. That counts the time of sleeping-in, of course."

"You just have to learn to relax whenever you can," said Edna.

"The day is all chopped up, even if you aren't on duty all the time," added Roy. "It's rough to get any consecutive time for important reading or studying or self-improvement."

I mentioned how interested I had been by their approach to democratic living in the orientation meetings, and asked them if it were difficult to make this work in practice.

"Where we run into problems," said Roy, "is when a teacher has been pretty autocratic with them before they come, or when there is a group that has been treated in a pretty autocratic way for quite a while. So they are not too willing or able to cope with democratic action.

"But you try it anyway?" I asked.

"Give them a taste of it, whether or not it's successful," said Edna. "Try to involve them in making decisions and choices."

"Try to get them to solve the problems themselves if possible," said Roy.

I noted that, if I remembered right, they had never mentioned "democracy" during the orientations.

"It doesn't help too much to talk a lot about democracy," said Roy.

"I think I talked more about it when I first started in the program," said Edna. "My emphasis now is just giving them a basis for solving their own problems later in the week. Make them think what they ought to do about a problem that might occur in the cabin. Give them an example. How can you solve that problem on your own — in a democratic way that would be fair to everyone? I think this is more useful than making out a list of rules."

I asked them about the discovery method of teaching that I had heard so much about, and had seen Roy practicing today, and was looking forward to seeing more of in the next two days. Was it difficult to teach that way? And what did they think of it?

"We have a tendency to teach the way we're taught," said Roy. "The discovery method wasn't one of the ways most of us were taught. You have to bite your tongue, really, to keep from telling them, and let them discover it. I'm convinced personally it is far less effective to say 'Look at that,' than to walk by and let them see it.

"One thing about it, though," he said after a moment, "you really have to wind yourself up with enthusiasm each morning, to use this method effectively. It's much easier to go out and tell them about the mistletoe, the moss, the fungus, and stop at each teaching station you have got used to, throughout the forest. My best hikes in rocks and minerals, or geology, are ones when I don't tell the children to look, there is a rock. But you've got to do this with a lot of enthusiasm. You've got to stoop over and get a rock yourself. They haven't picked one up yet, but they are all around you looking, and then you take it and break it and look at the colors. You are interested yourself. Then they head in every direction, looking for their own rocks. You don't tell them, 'Now, collect.' You lead them into it by doing it."

"I suspect half the children on a hike like that don't even realize they are discovering," said Roy. "No one *tells* them they're discovering."

"You walk by the Jeffrey pine until finally someone sees it," said Edna.

"Don't you waste a lot of time that way?" I asked.

"Not when you prime them with questions that lead them to discover the pine," said Edna. "Or discover something else equally interesting."

"I'm sold on it," said Roy. "I think they get more and it sinks deeper in the same unit of time."

They talked on about the importance of the teacher's own interest and enthusiasm. Roy told about an Audubon hike he went on once, where the guide must have done that hike several hundred times, but got interested in it as though he never had been there before in his whole life, so far as anyone could tell. "He had us all looking over his shoulder," Roy said. "We couldn't get enough of the experience."

I asked them what they thought the school camp program did for the children who took part in it.

"More awareness of the natural world," said Roy.

Edna said it taught responsibility.

"So many of them have never had a chance to be away from home at all and the camping experience is entirely new to them, and the idea of taking responsibility themselves," she said. "Something just as simple as brushing their teeth in the morning. At home they've been told to brush their teeth. Here there isn't someone to tell them to. At home there is somebody to pick up after them. Here they are expected to be responsible for making their beds, cleaning the cabin, doing the dishes, and things like that."

"It isn't just what we tell them," added Roy. "It's what everybody else is doing too. They just get in the swim of things. It isn't quite the same as if they are all by themselves. They bring this up constantly — the experience of living together."

"What do WE look like to the frog?"

"This is one of the things they always bring up in the Thursday night meeting," said Edna. "It seems to be one of the most important things to them, especially to the girls — getting to sleep in the same cabin with their friends."

I asked how well prepared the children usually were for the

camp experience. They said there were great differences in the preparation they had.

"But even when they are well prepared, it's a matter of the reality of experience," Roy said. "They study conservation in the classroom, and now they are actually up there bucking wood."

"Conservation is the one big project they all have in the classroom," Edna explained. "When they come later in the year, and all of them have had it in school, you can do lots more with them. You can relate conservation practices to the whole natural scene. It's more meaningful to them."

"And there's so much you can do by way of following this experience up in the classroom when they get back home," she said. "It fits into science, conservation, reading, creative writing and art, social studies . . ."

"They can get their material ready and present it to a PTA, or a school assembly, or a lower grade," Roy said. "They can put up their exhibits, and tie in library work."

By this time mountain air was having an effect, and two camp teachers and one visitor were beginning to grow sleepy. Edna wanted to set something right, though. "Let's not go off the deep end, and get the idea that the programmed activities and the classroom follow-up are the only places where the learning goes on," she said. "I'm not so sure that we don't have an opportunity to teach quite a bit even during shower time or clean-up time. You are an influence, there, and maybe an example."

"Now, what's the way home?"

Roy stopped me at the door to add an additional thought.

"Don't get the wrong idea from what we said about the lack of time for a teacher in camp," he said. "This is the only job I think I've ever had, and I've had quite a few of them, where you don't watch the clock to see whether quitting time has come. You watch the clock to see if you can possibly get in the things you want to do before you have to quit. You don't say you can't wait until 4 o'clock; you say, it's almost 4 o'clock already, and I'm ten minutes behind and I simply have to give them a taste of the contour maps or something like that. You always want *more* time with them, not less."

"Yes," said Edna, "it's that kind of job."

# VII
## LEARNING FROM THE DESERT

TUESDAY NIGHT, O-kah-gah, the Wet Wind, disdained the prayer at the Indian ceremony, and dropped three hours of rain on Camp Cuyamaca. When the camp awakened Wednesday, fog hung near the ground, and a soft wind, much warmer than the day before, moved through the valley spattering fine rain on the windows. Long before Harry announced it at breakfast, everyone knew that the all-day hikes would have to be cancelled. The woods would be too wet.

Disappointment hung over the cream of wheat, scrambled eggs, and raisin toast heaped on the breakfast tables. People looked less

The Wet Wind dropped three hours of rain on Camp Cuyamaca.

sleepy than on the previous morning. Walt reported that Northwind had been much quieter than Monday night, and someone remarked that even a steel mill would be quieter than Northwind was Monday night. Don said the Southwind boys had gone right off to sleep with only a minor skirmish, although in the middle of the night a boy got sick and threw up, and Don took him to Ill Wind. Isabel and Dottie said the girls' cabins were quiet, and everyone had got a lot of sleep. "Second night's always easier," Walt explained. The only sleepy looking staff member this morning was Carol the nurse. She said that the sick little boy from Don's cabin had kept on being sick for a couple of hours, and she had been up most of the night taking care of him.

Harry told the campers the schedule would be changed around, the hike would be set for Thursday. It might be necessary to have half-day, rather than all-day hikes; but they would definitely get out on hikes in the woods unless the weather got worse. "What do the Weatherbirds say?" he asked.

A tall girl with bangs down to her eyebrows rose to report for the Weatherbirds. She was a bit embarrassed, and the audience didn't let her forget the fair weather forecast of yesterday. She admitted that today, also, the Weatherbirds were somewhat puzzled. There seemed to be rain, and yet the barometer was rising. She predicted rain, and yet it might clear up. Tomorrow might be a good day. Or a bad day. Anyway, she concluded happily, the moisture sticks showed that the danger of forest fires was now only "medium low."

"How were things in Northwind last night?" I asked George.

"Pretty good," he said. "Quieter than Monday." He snickered a little, and looked at his cabin mates.

"What happened Monday?" I asked.

"Those boys' cabins are awful," said Maria, half enviously.

"Guys just didn't want to go to sleep," said George. "Everybody was a little wild. Wanted to goof off. Kind of excited, first night in camp."

"There were those two goof balls," said Yankees. "Monday night everyone was talking almost, but there was one boy from our school and one from La Mesa, and the one on the bottom bunk was from our school, and on the side of the wall where the window was, he would climb up and look over the bunk and say 'Hi, Freddie!' And everybody would start laughing. The top guy jumped off once, but Ernie stopped that."

"Was Ernie pretty rough with you?"

"No, he was nice. Probably should have whomped us."

"It was a long time before anybody got to sleep?"

"Yeah, when we all got sleepy, and some guys just wouldn't get quiet, Ernie finally sent one guy to the shower room."

"You got more sleep last night? Feel better?"

"Oh, yeah. Lots more. Went right to sleep."

I took another look at the fog and made some changes in my own schedule. The weather would probably be better at Camp Marston, on the other side of the mountains, they told me; and even if it wasn't, Marston had the desert trips, where it would be dry no matter what. And Edwin Pumala was coming to Camp Palomar for dinner, and tonight would be a good time for a talk with him. So this looked like my best chance to see something of what went on in the other camps. I packed a few things and warmed up the car.

Little George was coming out of kitchen duty.

"I'm going to learn fire-spotting today," he said. "Are you going to be in my class?"

"I can't," I said, "I've got to go up to the other camps."

"Can I go along with you?" he asked.

I told him I was afraid he couldn't, and he looked a little hurt.

"Be sure to write a letter to your daddy today," I said.

"Yeah, OK," he said. "Goodbye, Doc!"

I delayed long enough to hear the first minutes of the activity meeting. The classroom teachers reported another set of high grades for the condition of the girls' cabins. The boys were graded considerably lower. Westwind and Eastwind got 11.5 and 11.4, and pats on the back. Southwind got only 6.0 and was described as looking generally like a disaster area. But Northwind, the villains of yesterday's report, had risen to a very respectable score of 9.5.

There was a roar of approval from the Northwind boys, and politely skeptical glances from everyone else. When I found myself joining in the chorus of approval, I realized that I had become a kind of "subway alumnus" of Northwind. It was the *interesting* cabin. By common consent, it was the most "difficult" cabin. It contained most of the problem boys, and had the worst record for disobedience and noise. Yet when even Ernie talked about his experiences there, he spoke half-admiringly. "You can't tell from one minute to the next what's going to happen down there," he said. "They always have something new to pull." The girls' cabins were neat and well behaved. Southwind, the other boys' cabin, was blander and quieter. But Northwind was the cabin that people

"They were sighting over compass tables, triangulating make-believe fires."

talked about. There were more pranks to report, more stories to tell after one had been there. If there were more difficulties, there were also more boys one remembered. There was more sheer animal energy in Northwind than in the other cabins. You were often irritated by it, but couldn't help liking it. And so, like any other subway alumnus I smiled in pride as the score was announced.

Then I ducked out of the meeting, and drove into the fog, north on 79 around the mountain curves between Cuyamaca Peak and Stonewall, through a cloud deck, along the shores of the Cuyamaca reservoir where the remains of the fabulous Stonewall gold mine were faintly visible on a neck of land, past a sudden vista of desert scenery to the east, west to the picturesque town of Julian, and south into the mountains again, to Camp Marston.

The weather *was* better. As I came in I could see the whole camp, stretched along the slopes of a narrow valley, with a large pond feeding into a stream that wound among magnificent oaks and pines. The buildings were in the style of summer camps rather than CCC camps, and there seemed to be many small cabins for sleeping quarters rather than a few large barracks buildings as at Cuyamaca. But the general impression was the same, and the bustle of camp activities was the same.

Fifteen children were trekking out to the pond with seines and pans. Another group were sighting over compass tables, triangulating make-believe fires, and reporting locations back to make-believe ranger headquarters. Others were engaged in orienteering, an activity that has become an official sport in Europe, and is simpler but no less absorbing in the camps. The objective of these children was to locate eight cans that are buried in the ground just deep enough so that, when their general position is discovered, a little kicking and scuffing of the dirt will reveal the can. The youngsters were working in pairs, peering across hand compasses and pacing off distances. They would call back and forth: "You're sure you started right at the cypress?" "All right, then, 40 degrees. Have you got it right on 40? Tell me which way to move." "The compass needle keeps swinging." "Well, take an average." They seemed to be fascinated by the exercise. They would pace two chain lengths at 40 degrees, then three at 350, and when they found the can at that point would turn around and measure 3½ chains at 30 degrees—following some typewritten directions which seemed to be different for each pair. "Gee, this is fun," a boy said to me. "Would you move just a little? I think you may be standing on the can."

Another group was panning dirt, not for gold, but for scheelite, which they could identify by its glow under an ultraviolet lamp.

"Why does the scheelite separate out from the crushed rock when we pan it?"

"Do they ever find gold?" I asked a camp teacher. "Oh, yes," he said. "The big Stonewall mine was not far away, you know. They took two million dollars out of that mine."

I knew these same activities would go on at some time during the week at Cuyamaca, and wondered whether anyone here, like Dan, was chewing his pencil while drafting an appeal for a chance to demonstrate more responsible behavior.

I found Denver Fox having a cup of coffee in the dining hall with the head counselor at Camp Marston, a calm, firm-spoken, outdoor type whom everyone seemed to call Tom, although I noticed on the list that his real name was Warren Brown. I hadn't expected to see Denver here, but was glad of it, not least because he offered to take me down to the desert. Tom explained that I was too late to go with either the conservation crew or the desert trip, but that I could go with a geology class to the desert rim that afternoon, and they could find a bed for me if I could stay the night. Denver said he wanted to get down to the desert anyway, and if I wanted to ride along with him we could catch up with the morning group, spend some time with them, and come back for lunch.

We drove ten miles or so, back through Julian, and down through a deep cut in the mountain toward the desert. Denver kept pointing out old gold mines. He said there was a time when the town of Julian, with its mining population, was nearly as large as San Diego, and in fact had come within a few votes of being made the county seat. We were riding along the Elsinore Fault, he said, pointing out a mountain escarpment at the left and outcroppings of the Julian Schist, the rock in which most of the gold was found. I asked him what we would have missed of the desert class, by this time, and this turned out to be a rare and rather wonderful opportunity to see how a master teacher looks at the process of outdoor education.

Denver said he didn't know, of course, exactly how these particular teachers had done it, but he would expect that they would stop at the top of the grade and let the children have a good look around them and note the kinds of trees, bushes, ground cover, rocks, soil, and birds or animals they could see. Then as they drove down toward the desert, they would be encouraged to note the changing scenery around them. As we drove, I began to see cottonwoods and sycamores, and then desert junipers, instead of mountain oaks and pines. Sage and cactus were appearing beside the road, and the ground was increasingly bare and sandy. Even in this drop of 2500 feet or so, said Denver, we would pass through quite different ecological zones, and the teacher would use them to prime the children with questions for which they could seek answers: Why does the scenery change? Bushes seem to be replacing trees: Why, and what is the difference between a tree and a bush? And so forth.

We saw Camp Marston's yellow school bus parked beside the road and pulled in behind it. We were on a bit of sandy tableland perhaps 200 feet above the main desert. Somewhere down below us, 25 sixth graders were hidden from our sight by dunes or underbrush.

Here the class would probably stop again, said Denver, for a long look around and some discussion of what they see. This is a desert: What distinguishes a desert from the kind of country they are used to? What makes it a desert? For instance, would the wall of mountains where they came from have any effect on the rain? How can they best study a desert? And what do they want to know about it, anyway?

This seemed to me to be the basic chemistry of learning that the school camps try to bring about: encourage children to be alert and curious about their natural environments, and to ask good questions; then to seek answers, and be alert to evidence that might provide the answers. This is what I saw happening again and again, and what Denver was teaching me by example that morning on the desert.

One of the first questions that would be likely to come up, he said, would be, how can plants survive in a desert climate? The obvious next step would be to examine some of the plants nearby to see how *they* have adapted to conditions. What does the tough skin of the cactus, for example, have to do with its ability to store moisture? How has the cactus developed so as to defend itself against hungry desert animals? (The thick skin? The needles?) How does the juniper protect itself? (Smell its leaves.) *Is* there any evidence of animals on the desert, by the way? This is the kind of questioning, leading to observation and problem-solving, that they hope will come out of an experience like this.

We walked down to the desert proper. From a distance it looked deceptively smooth. Close up it was rocky and uneven, with dunes

"What did the Indians use to grind in these morteros?"

and ridges, juniper and cactus, that could and did hide 25 children less than a quarter of a mile away. In the half-sun of that Wednesday morning the pastel colors of the desert were unbelievably beautiful. We looked over brickish shades of tan and red and lemon yellow to mountains that were almost lavender. And then we came around a little rocky knob, and saw the class in front of us.

They looked like the same kind of children and wore the same kind of clothes I had got used to at Cuyamaca. Their jackets and sweaters of red, green, blue, and orange stood out from the pastels of the desert. A few of the boys had on caps or hats; most of the girls were bare-headed, and their long hair fell around their shoulders. They were showing some of the same excitement I had seen on the hike at Cuyamaca when the children had found the Indian village.

These children, too, had come upon signs of Indian habitation. They had picked up pieces of ollas, and found bowl-like depressions worn into rocks. When we arrived, they had found also some smooth grinding stones and were fitting them into the bowl-like places.

Now the camp teacher was making use of the fact that they knew they were on the site of an ancient winter home of Indians. "Close your eyes," he was saying. He was a tall blonde young man in light blue jacket. "It's a long time ago. Imagine that you are Indians. You live here. You look over there to the east and you see a trail of dust. What is it?"

"An old Indian fighter. I've got my arrows ready," said one boy.

"Pony Express," suggested another.

They suggested it might be the white settlers coming. Covered wagons. The Mormon battalion. The prospectors.

"How did the Indians use this plant?"

"All these people coming in," said the teacher. "How would you feel? Are you Indians happy? Are you concerned?"

They talked about that, and then changed from history to every-day problems.

"How many of you are hungry?" asked the teacher. The answer was predictable; 12-year-olds seem to be hungry most of the time.

"What will we eat?" he asked. "Remember we are Indians. What is there to eat here?"

They looked around. Let's shoot some animals. What animals? With what? How could the Indians have caught or killed desert animals? They talked about snares and traps, and stone axes. What roots, or herbs, or berries could the Indians eat? They tenta-tively sampled a few berries and leaves, and talked about the in-side of the cactus being soft and edible. How could they get it out? It seemed it was possible to build a fire, roast the cactus, and pull out the inside. They talked a bit about what the Indians knew of preserving fruits like the wild apricot.

"What are we going to drink? Where can we find water?"

You could see that the children were challenged by this; they were putting themselves in the place of the native Californians who had lived here before the white man. But the lesson they were being taught was something more general than how the In-dians lived. It was the whole question of adaptation to environ-ment? How does man do it? How do plants and animals do it?

"Anybody still hungry?" asked the teacher. "Then I guess we had better think about lunch in the twentieth century," he said with a smile.

Lunch at Camp Marston was good and plentiful, and there were reports on the morning activities and compliments to the conser-vation group. After lunch, Denver went into a conference with Tom, and I climbed into the bus and went to the desert rim.

The camp teacher in charge of this activity was named George. He was a large, husky young man, with a round face, a wispy light brown Falstaffian moustache that curved around his mouth, a res-onant bass voice, and a merry laugh. A teacher aide named Nate was assisting him, and his class consisted of 15 children and me.

We rode through Julian again toward the desert, but turned off the road before it began to descend to the desert. We parked the bus and sat and talked a few minutes about what geology was and what geologists did. "Why do people want to study the earth?" asked George, after they had agreed that geology was the study of the earth. They answered that very well — to build on it, to find valuable minerals, to learn about the history of it. "Is it important to know the history?" asked George, and when he got the expected

"Is this rock radioactive?"

answer, he said, "It's not only important, but it's kind of fun, isn't it?"

"When we talk about geological history, what units of time are we talking about?" he asked. They knew it was millions of years. Then he asked, "All right, now how can we study these millions of years of history of the earth? How does a scientist do it? He looks, they said. He takes samples. He analyzes and measures them. He digs. "Good," said George. "Now we can't measure very much today, but we can look, and we can raise questions, and we can collect samples and examine them and think about them." He gave them each a pad, and told them to write down the questions that occurred to them as they walked along. "We aren't going to have to stay in a single-file line," he said. "You can spread out a bit, just so you don't wander out by yourself where you can't see anybody else, because it's pretty easy to get lost here too. But I want you to explore. Observe. Take samples. And the main thing: to write down in these notebooks about what you see. Then later we'll stop and talk about these questions and look at some of your samples. Now let's get out of this warm old bus."

We walked a few hundred yards out to the desert rim. It was a magnificent sight. Half a mile below us, the pastel desert stretched to the horizon, interrupted every 15 or 20 miles by a range of lavender mountains. Behind the second range was a line of blue, and

George asked them whether they knew what it was. They guessed it: The Salton Sea. "Can we go there?" a small boy asked. "How far do you guess it is?" George asked. They decided it was 40 or 50 miles. Far beyond that the desert reached away toward the Arizona border.

We fanned out and strolled along the rim. Occasionally a child stopped to write something in his pad. They scuffed rocks with their feet, bent down and fingered them, began to pick up huge quantities of samples. One girl found a discarded teapot, and carried it along with her. It was soon filled to overflowing with rocks, and she discarded some to collect new ones. A girl asked about some lichen, and they talked about how lichen helps decompose rocks into soil, and what other forces also do that. A boy brought

"How did these rocks get turned up like this?"

a piece of mica for George to look at. "What's this rock?" he asked. After it was identified, they talked about the difference between a rock and a mineral, and decided that mica was a mineral. But the first major stop came when someone called attention to some outcropping of rock which seemed to run about 70 degrees from the horizontal.

"Wow!" he said.

"Have you seen some of that in the ground as you were walking along?" George asked.

"No," they said doubtfully.

"No?" said George. "Look, here's some of it over here. What is this strange looking stuff?"

"Sand?"

"Why do you say it's sand?"

"Something must give you a hint."

"Maybe this was the desert once. Or the ocean."

George wanted them to come to that answer by a different road. So he said, "Why don't you all come a little closer and we'll have a look." They gathered in a tight circle. "Take a piece of this. Feel it a little bit. What does it feel and look like?"

"Sand."

"It's too hard for sand."

"It's sedimentary rock," said a roundish boy, who wore a tan sweater and had pulled a white Navy hat down over his ears. "It's formed by things falling on top of it and getting squished together."

"Sedimentary rock!" said George as though in surprise. "Does everybody here know what that is? . . . Maybe you can explain it to us," he said to the boy with the white hat.

"Well . . . uh . . . ah," said the boy. "It's layers. It's all different sorts of things. Mud, dirt, sand that's settled down to the bottom of something. Like a liquid. It just sits there, and layer after layer goes on top of it. And then it squeezes together real tight."

Obviously, I thought, this boy knows. But George wanted more information.

"Where does it come from?" he asked, and directed the question to the girl with the teapot.

"Rain pushes it. And rivers."

"And where does it come from before that? It has to have a source."

"What do you mean by source?" asked someone after a little pause. "You mean, what it's made of?"

"Where did it come from before it started to the ocean?"

"The land." "Soil."

"Soil?" said George. "And where does soil come from?"

"Rocks."

"So you think this may have been rocks that have broken down. How could they break down?"

"Oh, you know," said a girl rather impatiently, "the stuff we were talking about back there—lichen, water, wind, and things."

George was pleased. They had passed his little review test.

"And how did you say it got down to the ocean after it was broken up into soil?"

"Rivers."

"Streams."

"But if you took some of this stuff and put it in a jar of water and it settled down to the bottom, not much would happen, would it?"

"No, 'cause there's not enough weight on it."

"Not enough weight?"

"And it's not there long enough."

"You mean this takes a long time?" asked George.

"Long enough to get all that weight on it and squeeze it down."

"How thick do you suppose this layer of sediment might be?"

They guessed miles, half a mile, quarter of a mile.

"Suppose we say it's 4,000 feet thick," said George. "These layers of sediment in this rock have built up for so many years that they are 4,000 feet thick. That's a pretty good bunch of sediment, isn't it?"

"Whew!"

"What would that sediment be like at the bottom?"

"All gooshy and mud."

"You think it would be mud?"

"Nah," said the boy with the white hat. "It would be solid."

"Why?"

"All that weight on it."

"Do you think if you were under 4,000 feet of sand and mud you might be . . . pretty solid?" George laughed his merry laugh, and they with him.

"But wait a minute!" George said. "If this rock was once on the bottom of the ocean, does that mean that there was once an ocean over the tops of these mountains?"

That set them thinking a minute. "Yes," one of them said tentatively.

"How did it get here?"

"Just came up."

There was some talk about that, and then a girl said decisively, "No, there wasn't an ocean here. It's too high. The land raised up."

"You mean these mountains haven't always been here?" asked George.

"No."

"What did this land look like, then, millions of years ago?"

"Water."

"You mean this was lower here?"

"It was low, and water was over it."

"How did the land rise up, then?"

A girl advanced a theory: "Well, the wind blows from another part of the ocean, and some of the sand stirs up, and it settles down in one spot, and gets to be a mountain."

"A mountain of sand 5,000 feet high?" asked George.

"Oh, nuts!" said a boy.

"How do *you* think the mountains were formed?" George asked him.

"Well, inside the earth there's all this pressure, and if there's a little crack all the lava and everything else starts pouring out, and pushes things up. If there's a fault, it slides it up."

"What do you think about that theory?" George asked them. They talked a bit about faults and volcanoes and magma and lava. George asked them to think about what forces there must be in the earth if they push up mountains like this. Then he said:

"Is there any way we can test this theory by what we can see here?"

"Have you looked carefully at these rocks here?" he asked, after a little silence.

"Yes, they're all slanted."

"Slanted?"

"They're all at an angle."

"Let's walk over here where we can see this outcrop closely. Let's look at it a minute. Now how did you say sedimentary rock would look if you looked at it?"

"It would be layers."

"All right. This rock is in layers, isn't it? How would these layers lie on the floor of the ocean?"

"What do you mean?"

"What caused the valley between the mountains?"

"If you took a knife and cut down through them while they were on the bottom of the ocean, how would they look?"

"They'd be flat," said the boy with the white hat.

"Then how come these layers seem to be tilted almost straight up?" asked George.

They saw it now. "Because something pushed them up," they said. "The forces in the earth. Pushed them up and made the mountain."

"So that too seems to agree with our theory," said George. "If something had pushed them up, they would be tilted, wouldn't they?"

They walked along, picking up rocks and feeling them, looking at the Elsinore fault and the mountain wall beside it that rose like a crouching lion from the desert floor. Every once in a while one of the boys or girls brought a rock to George or Nate, and often a little knot of them gathered to talk about it. George showed them an old gold mine, boarded up. There was some gold in it, he said, but the chief product they were mining was scheelite, which is the ore of tungsten. He asked them what tungsten is used for, and they knew one use: the filaments of electric lights. "Can we go in the mine?" asked a boy. "Do you think we ought to take the chance of a thousand tons of rock falling on us?" asked George. "We'd be sedimentary!" said a little girl, and we all laughed together as groups laugh over their own private jokes.

They looked down the fault line and talked about how great changes occur at the weakest places in the earth's crust (dishes and glass break where there's a crack, they noted) and how earthquakes happen. And at the end, they all sat down with their samples and questions. George told them they would have to leave at once if they were going to get back for play hour, but perhaps they would prefer to use the time to talk over their samples. Their protests over missing play ("George, how could you!") were more in fun than earnest, and a boy expressed the group consensus when he said they should use the time on the samples and George should tell them a longer story at bedtime.

"First, then, let's remember what we have found out about how this place got to look the way it does," said George. "Before there were mountains here there was what?"

"An ocean."

"Right. A few million years ago there was an ocean, the same ocean we know today in San Diego, over all this land and far to the east. The Salton Sea is like a little puddle left over from it. If we had been writing these questions down here a few million years ago, we'd have had to use scuba gear."

They all laughed together.

"It was all flat. Then what happened?"

"The forces down in the earth pushed up some of the land."

"Right. We saw the old sea bottom standing up on end. And now what's happening?

"Is anything happening to these rocks around us now?" he prodded them, when there was no answer.

"They're breaking down into soil."

"Right. And the rain and the streams are carrying the soil down to the sea and the lakes, and over a long time they will form sedimentary rock. So, in a way, it's all happening again, isn't it? As time goes on, would you expect these mountains to get rounder and lower, or higher and sharper?"

Rounder and lower, they said.

"Right, because they are being worn off and carried down to the lowlands and the sea. Would you guess, then, the Appalachian Mountains that have round peaks are younger or older than the Sierra, where the peaks are sharper and craggier?"

Older, they said.

"Other things being equal, they ought to be older," George said. "The earth is always changing, but not very fast, is it? Can we count on these mountains being here next week, after we go home from camp?"

Oh, yes, they said.

"Can we count on them being here 50 million years from now?"

They were uncertain about that.

"Yes, we would be pretty doubtful about that," said George. "Now let's see your samples."

As they talked about the rocks, George began to put them in three piles. One was the sedimentary rocks, the sandstone and shale. They all knew what this kind of rock was and how it got to be. The second pile was igneous rocks, and they soon recognized that these must be the very hard stuff that came out of the hot interior of the earth. And they had no trouble answering George's question as to why they found igneous and sedimentary rocks together: The igneous stuff came up from deep in the earth and helped push up the flat land into mountains. But there was a third pile of rocks which was not like either of the others. George urged them to look at these rocks and feel them and see what they could tell about them. They took turns handling pieces of schist and quartzite. They noted that these rocks seemed to have lines like the sedimentary rocks, and yet looked and felt different. For one thing, they were harder than the sandstone or shale.

"Could these be sedimentary rocks that something has happened to?" George asked.

"Yes," they agreed.

"What could have happened?"

"Could they have got hot?" asked the boy with the white hat.

"How could that have happened?"

"Maybe they got against the hot stuff boiling up?"

"Right," said George with real pleasure. "That's what happened. This is that same sedimentary rock that underwent heat and pressure and fused together until it made a quite different kind of rock. Even this schist here — Tommy, show them that piece of Julian schist you have there — it has been changed enough to make it harder, and make it feel kind of slippery."

"That's right," Tommy said. "It *does* look like it, but it's harder, and it *does* feel slippery."

When I left them they were still examining rocks that had been made 50 million years in the past. I had to get to Camp Palomar in time for dinner an hour in the future.

# VIII
# EVOLUTION OF AN AREAWIDE CAMPING PROGRAM

FROM MARSTON TO PALOMAR you drive mostly north and west, down out of the mountains to the plateau land again, through the Santa Ysabel Indian Reservation, between low mountains and mesas where occasionally a path turns off marked "Jeep Trail," past Lake Henshaw, over fairly level roads until you come to Mount Palomar itself. Then you take a road that twists and turns and ties itself in knots as it climbs a granite shoulder of the mountain. You come around a turn and get a fleeting glimpse of most of southern California—south to the Mexican border, north to Orange County, west to the islands in the sea far beyond San Diego. When you reach the end of the climb you turn 90 degrees away from the Observatory road, down into the Palomar State Park where Camp Palomar sits at the edge of deep woods on the slopes of a broad and lovely valley.

In many ways Camp Palomar is the handsomest of the camps. Cuyamaca sits between mesas, and Marston in rolling country, but Palomar is definitely in mountain scenery. It is higher in altitude than the other camps, and the exciting views are closer at hand. The buildings themselves are neither more nor less attractive than those at the other camps, although the staff quarters at Palomar somewhat resemble a mountainside Swiss chalet and are very handsome, indeed. From the buildings a half mile of tree-lined meadow slopes down to the creek, the pond, and the park road. The mountain meadow at Palomar is something one remembers for a long time.

Th head counselor at Palomar is a solid, sturdy-looking man, with reddish hair and moustache who, in the first name tradition of the camps, is called John. His last name is Craine. He gave me a quick tour of the camp while we waited for dinner and Edwin Pumala. The dormitories at Palomar, with the exception of one old CCC building that holds 30, are considerably smaller than those at Cuyamaca. Most of them have sleeping quarters for 10 children, one for 16. The girls' cabins are clustered together in the woods, and the boys' cabins clustered at another place, and each group has a separate toilet and shower building. At Palomar the cabins are named after planets and trees, as at Cuyamaca they are named for winds, and at Marston for rocks and chaparral. As at the other camps, there is an infirmary, where a nurse presides over minor ills. Palomar has old buildings of a CCC vintage which are used

96

for crafts shops and classrooms.

I asked John how he perceived the differences in the camps. He said that the natural environment of Camp Palomar was considerably different from the others. For one thing, Palomar is more remote; the nearest community is an hour's drive. Then, he said, the ride up the mountain and the scenery at Palomar are quite impressive to children. "If you would see them get off the bus, you would realize it," he laughed. "When they arrive here, they realize, or begin to realize, that they are in the mountains!"

"Of course, one of the big differences here," he added, "is that we have the observatory so near us. I would judge that even though these children live only perhaps 70 miles from the observatory, on the average 80 per cent or more have never been there. So they are eager to go. And every child at camp gets to visit it, weather conditions permitting."

He said that there was necessarily a certain amount of physical determinism that helped shape the program at Palomar as at the other camps. Palomar has the observatory, but it is too far away to take the desert trips as at Marston. It has excellent facilities for different types of conservation experience, but it doesn't emphasize the Indian program, as at Cuyamaca. "Cuyamaca has more of the history of the Indians at hand," John said. "There were Indians here, but you don't find the arrow-makers' villages as at Cuyamaca."

The fact that Camp Palomar has small sleeping cabins makes it important, as at Marston, to place special emphasis on developing responsible behavior and pride in the living groups, because it would be infeasible to have a teacher present all the time in each cabin. Because the Palomar craft shops and classroom areas are smaller than those at Cuyamaca, it makes it necessary to have a type of schedule in which a great many different kinds of activities, participated in by small groups, go on every day. Cuyamaca, on the other hand, he said, has enough room that it can schedule most of its crafts activities one day, its science activities another day, and so forth.

The programs at the three school camps are basically similar, he said, and are aimed at giving the children the same general kind of experiences, but the resources available at the different camps make it desirable to go about it a bit differently.

I asked him how long he had been with the school camp program. Fifteen years, he said. He came into the program as a teacher at Palomar when Denver Fox was principal at Cuyamaca. In John's second year in the program, Tom Brown, now the head counselor at Marston, became head counselor at Palomar, and

John served two years under Tom. All the present heads of the instructional program — Denver Fox, the principal, Tom Brown at Marston, Harry Bryce at Cuyamaca, and John Craine at Palomar — had come into the school camps in the late 1940's or at the beginning of the 50's, and had been working together under Denver's guidance to shape the program for nearly 20 years. I asked John what kinds of change he had seen in that time. He said that a great deal had changed, but it had been gradual. Denver had been the great force in developing the instructional program. The most significant change, he felt, was the development and use, through trial and error and constant evaluation, of the problem-solving, scientific, "discovery" method used in the school camps. "I am convinced," he said, "it is the best approach to develop inquisitive minds, alert, thinking human beings."

I asked him how they made sure that their new teachers learned to use that approach. He said it was principally by means of inservice training — nearly three weeks at the beginning of the year, and constant inservice during the year. At the beginning of the year, he said, the entire teaching staffs of the three camps spend approximately a week at Cuyamaca, the same at Palomar, and then nearly a week at whichever camp they have been assigned to. During that time, much of the burden of teaching falls on the experienced staff. These people provide actual work and learning experience in the different areas. For instance, they go out on a conservation assignment, using the same approach with the new teachers as with the children. They go through the experience of pond biology or a field hike, just as they would with the children, using the same problem-solving, discovery approach. Some new teachers catch on a bit sooner, of course; their backgrounds and experience have something to do with it. This same thing, he said, is true of learning our democratic approach to cabin living. After all, how many people are familiar with this type of approach? And so it is not surprising, he said, that a teacher in the outdoor education program is not as efficient as he could be until he has been in the school camps a year.

Edwin Pumala arrived, and we began to talk about other things. Pumala is a tall man, with some white around his temples, an outdoor complexion, warmth and dignity of manner. He spoke with a quiet eloquence. I had rather expected a salesman, a spellbinder, or a political type. Something like this, I imagined, might have been necessary to keep a complex, publicly supported program like this one going for 20 years. But he was calm and thoughtful, rather than aggressive or noisy. He spoke like a man who was confident both of the rightness of his position and of be-

Palomar — "How does the telescope follow a star long enough to take a picture of it?"

ing able to get a fair hearing for it.

At dinner (the same good food and substantial menus seemed to prevail throughout the school camps) while he did his business with John, I listened to the reports of the Palomar observatory trip that bubbled up from the children around me. I gathered that before they went to the observatory they had examined a model of the great 200-inch telescope, and talked about how it worked and what it was used for. Then they had ridden over to the observatory and spent about 45 minutes in the museum looking mostly at pictures taken at Palomar, of galaxies and neublae and planets, and finally another 45 minutes or so looking through the observation windows at the great telescope itself. They heard a brief talk about it, and, I judged, had plenty of questions to ask of the teachers that accompanied them. As a result of examining the model, however, they knew where to look for the mirror housing and the place where the pictures themeselves were taken, and the place where the astronomer would be, and how the timing apparatus worked, and a great many such facts which would be new to the average visitor to the observatory.

They were excited over what they had seen; there was no doubt of that. The great spiral nebula which has been so beautifully photographed at Palomar was variously called Andromeda, Androdema, Andronema, and Andromena, but they knew something about it. And their imaginations were stimulated to raise ideas and questions about how anyone could measure how far away it was, and whether our galaxy looks anything like it, and how many planets like the earth there might be in Andromeda — or was it Andromena? One little girl asked whether it wasn't true that the Palomar telescopes couldn't see half the heavens around us, and was there a big telescope like this south of the equator too? She said she would like to go down and see what they could see there. She and many of the others sat there thinking the long, the faraway thoughts that have led man always to ask what is over the next hill, beyond the ocean, over the curves of earth?

After dinner, Pumala and I sat in the gathering twilight and talked for an hour about school camping.

"What made the difference in San Diego?" I asked him. "Why did school camping work out so well here?"

"There are a number of good school camps elsewhere," he said. "There must be a hundred in California alone. Camp Tyler, Texas, is one that people often mention. But I think the advantage we had in San Diego right from the beginning was a tremendously broad base of community support. I have read the minutes of the very first meetings, long before I came, and there have been at least 20 community groups at those meetings. It was very comparable to the New England town meeting. All these people and organizations came together and looked at how to give some outdoor experiences to children.

"Out of this came some practical suggestions. First they made an inventory of areas in San Diego County that were owned by the federal government or the state or the county and could be made into camps. They found one that was supposedly owned by the Army Engineers, who had given it to the State Parks. But before the community people could do anything about it they knew they had to have some official status, so the ordinance of 1943 was passed, creating a camp commission to which all these community organizations were in an advisory capacity. Once the organization was established they made an investigation and were able through the help of Assemblymen and Senators to get a five-year lease on Camp Cuyamaca. This itself is an interesting story — the play of politics and community action and the state's reaction

to it — but the point is that these groups worked together. You
didn't have the schools and the politicians and the community organizations going their separate directions. They banded together."

"How did *you* come into it?" I asked.

"The new commission went to the Kellogg Foundation to get
help," he said. "They heard that the Foundation had an outdoor
education program before the war. Mr. Kellogg was always deeply
interested in children. The Foundation sent Dr. Hugh Masters out
to give a talk in San Diego. He was such an inspirational speaker
that they again called on the Kellogg Foundation to help them get
the program started. It happened at a time when I was just getting
out of the Coast Guard. The Foundation suggested I come here and
talk to the people of the commission. I was so taken by all this
community enthusiasm that I didn't even ask questions about
money, but accepted the responsibility to get the program started.
One of the first and best things I did was to get probably as good a
man as could be found, who was imbued with the idea that outdoor experiences for children were worthwhile. His name was Bill
Goodall, and he is now director of the Audubon Society of the
Western States. He came out here with his family as the director
of Camp Cuyamaca. That is the way it got started on March 17,
1946.

"But you can't credit me and you can't credit Goodall," he said.
"You've got to credit San Diego. The thing that makes any program
sound is when people get so involved, emotionally and intellectu-
ally, that it's their program. This is the way the people felt, and
this is the way the community is. The schools in San Diego have
many such community programs. Now the TV station has come
into being, and all the cultural agencies, the colleges, the public
schools, the parochial schools, are working together making a San
Diego County TV station — not a San Diego State College station,
not a parochial school station, not a private station, but a *community* TV station — an educational station that went on the air
in February. That is the San Diego spirit."

"First you called it a Recreation Commission, then a Recreation
and Camping Commission, and finally a Camping Commission,
didn't you?" I said. "Does that represent an evolution in your
thinking about it?"

"It was more of a camping program at first," he said, "because
the leadership was not trained in science and some of those other
areas we emphasize now. It was more exploring and having a happy living situation. It was Indian lore and getting to know the area
around the camp. Much of the routine of camp that was estab-

lished in those early years still lasts. Certainly, though, there has been a change toward making it a school camp."

"An educational experience?"

"What we are actually doing is exposing the child to a different world of environment and attempting, during the week he is up there, to bring it into focus in such a way that it is meaningful for him, trying to get him to be curious about it and think about it. That is an educational experience."

I told him that I wished someone had introduced me to geology, when I was in the sixth grade, as I had heard some children introduced to it today, or to astronomy as these Palomar youngsters were being introduced to it. He smiled in agreement.

"But who is to say what is the really big experience of that week in camp?" he asked. "Conservation, outdoor science, social living experience — all those fit together so closely that you can't say one or the other is more important. Who is to say, maybe for some kid coming up from a minority group, that the big experience of camp isn't simply an experience with the other groups? Or for the more fortunate youngster, coming into contact with minority groups and being awakened to the fact that they are more like him than different?

"You mustn't lose sight of the fact that this program was sold first on the idea of community camping, not school camping," he said. "I don't think the Camping Commission would have inspired anywhere near the efforts they have aroused if we hadn't had the idea of camping for the entire community. When the school children weren't there, other community groups would use the facility, as they do on weekends now, and in the summer.

"In the summer," he added, "we run a camp for the children who aren't in organized camping or youth groups, like the Scouts and YMCA. We run camps for the crippled children, the retarded children, even the blind children. We have children of welfare families at a camp, and special interest groups like the Safety Patrol and the music camp."

"Tell me about the Safety Patrol camp," I said. "I have heard a lot about it."

"Yes," he said. "I think the Safety Patrol in San Diego — school youngsters who supervise the crossings — dates back more than 30 years. Up until two years ago they never had had an accident on a crossing supervised by the Patrol. Ten San Diego policemen teach safety to school children all year, and cooperate with the Patrol. Kids come into the Patrol, many of them, in the fourth grade, and stay on in the fifth and sixth, and all that time they see the policeman as a policeman. Then they go to camp in the summer, and the policeman takes off his uniform and acts just like dad at home. Most of these policemen become friends of the Patrol boys, and they stay friends as long as they live."

"You have camping programs, then, the year around?" I said.

"Yes, at Cuyamaca and Palomar. Marston we only rent in the winter."

"Tell me the story of getting the Cuyamaca lease from the State Park Commission," I said. "You mentioned it before."

He laughed. "That happened before I came to San Diego, and the story has been handed down to me by members of the Commission who were there in the first years. The story they tell is that when they found out who owned Camp Cuyamaca, they asked to be on the agenda of the State Park Commission which was about to meet at Cuyamaca. The general feeling of the Park Commission was they didn't want to set a precedent of letting city and county bodies rent park lands, but they let the San Diego group have a place on the agenda. About 25 or 30 people drove up to Cuyamaca on a cold winter day. They were told they would appear in the afternoon, and there wasn't any place for them to stay, so they went into what was to be Camp Cuyamaca — the old CCC buildings — with no fire in the buildings, no lunch or anything, and stayed there until 3 o'clock, and by that time they were nearly frozen and fit to be tied. This was a group of community leaders, remember, including the superintendents of city and county schools and some of the most prominent individuals in San Diego. Then the Park Commission sent word that the agenda was so tight the San Diego representatives could not be heard that day. This was about 3 o'clock in the afternoon, remember. They said, if you come tomorrow to Borrego, which was 60 miles farther from San Diego, we'll try to get to the San Diego Problem.

"So all these people went back home, not very happy. They decided they were going to be there the next day, regardless. They called around and got some more people to come with them, so altogether about 50 people drove to the meeting in Borrego, about 130 miles. There was some delay at Borrego, too, but Leo Carillo who was a member of the State Park Commission and also a citizen of San Diego County, said 'I think this has gone far enough; let us give this delegation the courtesy of being heard.' So they heard the San Diego request that they lease the campsite in Cuyamaca Park, and finally Mr. Carillo made the motion and it was seconded and passed to give them a five-year lease. It was a kind of understanding, though not written, that the lease would not be renewed. The Park Commission could see all the communities of California coming after their land. I don't believe they were hostile to the idea of children going to camp or anything like that; they were a new commission, and felt the responsibility to preserve the wild parts of California for posterity. The fact that the lease *was* extended after five years indicated that some members of the Park Commission came to feel differently than at first."

"As I understand it," I said, "there are really three employers at the camps. There is the County civil service that hires the cooks and maintenance men and so forth, and also the San Diego City schools and the La Mesa-Spring Valley schools. Can you explain that to me?"

"You might say it has evolved out of experience," Pumala said. "There was no pattern to follow because we had the complicated

"Half the time the kids don't even know they're discovering."

cooperation of so many agencies. The first thought was that we should charge enough so that the people who went to the camps would pay for the program. So at first all of our people were people employed by the County. It wasn't long before the schools saw the weakness in this arrangement: They weren't entirely satisfied with the kind of leadership the counselors were providing. They realized that one had to pay for the kind of leadership they wanted. The city schools were very adamant on this matter, and when they saw that the Camp Commission did not have the funds to pay for that kind of leadership, they said, all right, we will contribute so many teachers and principals. It worked out that the teachers would be credentialed teachers, and the camp principal would be an elementary school principal. That was when

Bill Goodall, whose background was in recreation rather than education, went into another position, and Denver Fox came in as principal, and has been here ever since.

"Finally, the Commission and the city schools both decided that if there were County schools participating in the program they should share the expenses, and the County superintendent and the superintendents of several of the county systems agreed, and their boards saw the logic of the situation, and the La Mesa-Spring Valley schools were asked to represent the county systems and hire some of the camp teachers. So now we have three employers — the County, the San Diego City School District, and the La Mesa-Spring Valley School District, and the latter two of these employ 35 to 40 people who are in charge of the instruction.

"Let me add," he said, "that we ask the parents only to pay what they would be responsible for anyway — food, clothing, sleeping equipment of their children, and so forth. It was understood from the first that the cost of instruction would be paid for by the schools, and the cost of maintenance would be paid for by the Commission and the schools. As you know, it costs parents $18.60 to send a child to the school camp for a week, and if a family doesn't think it can pay that, usually one of the organizations cooperating in the campership program can pick it up, and nobody knows the difference."

I asked him whether it took any special legislation to make the school camp program possible.

"We found in the case of some counties that the county district attorney refused to pay any money to school camps because the school code did not give him that authority," Pumala said. "Our county felt that there was authority, but to make sure of it we asked for legislation to make it legal to transport school children beyond the boundaries of a district and to work out property leases for camps, and such things. Fortunately the reaction was so wholehearted in support of school camping that the state legislature passed it almost without objection, and Governor Warren signed it, and it became a part of the school code and is to this day.

"Also," he said, "we have asked for and obtained legislation to let us sign a long enough lease for camp sites so that we can sell the 1.5 million dollars worth of bonds voted by San Diego County to let us construct new buildings at Cuyamaca and Palomar. That's all the legislation."

'I understand you once had a Grand Jury investigation of the camping program," I said.

He winced a little, and then smiled his craggy smile.

"A Grand Jury investigation," he said, "is like a war — a very fine experience to come through successfully, but you never want to go through it again. The Camp Commission grew like Topsy. We were forced to make decisions and carry out assignments without any rule book to follow. So we did many things that no other department in the County of San Diego had ever done before. The Grand Jury investigation had to do with a charge made by one of the members of the staff — an emotionally involved camp counselor who in a quick decision wrote a letter to the Grand Jury and the Jury called him and his witnesses in. Out of it came some charges about how we were conducting the program that had nothing to do with the program or the children or criminal action by anyone. The original charge was quickly dissipated, when it was found to be entirely false. I think one reason why the outcome was so favorable was that no one was trying to hide anything. Yet, those of us who were involved reacted as human beings do, and it was a rough experience, and as I look back at it now I know that I grew a great deal in ability to react to situations more maturely.

"Anyway, there was a charge about poor administration, doing things that were not provided for in the rules. I am the first one to say that there *was* poor administration. But it was a result of the fact that we didn't have money enough, facilities enough, leadership enough. We were just a 'have not' organization trying to do a job in a manner that would give youngsters an experience so wonderful that the community would want it to happen over and over again. The heart-warming thing was that parents came to the defense of the program wherever the Grand Jury investigated. Even though we were running a program of about a million dollars a year there was no evidence in the audit of dishonesty or inconsistency or manipulation of funds or resources or anything of the kind. Merely of doing things that were not specifically in the county code, or trying to trust one's memory farther than perhaps one should. Anyway, it came out all right, and after the investigation and the Jury recommendations, the Camp Commission went ahead quietly and put into practice the recommendations that were made.

"On the whole I think we have been very fortunate," he said. "I don't know any program that is so much in the limelight where it could be challenged. Just think, any week, the 400 to 450 children at our camps could come home and say, what a terrible time they had at camp. At the end of every week, the classroom teachers make an evaluation, the children make an evaluation, and more important than that is what they tell their parents.

How long do you think this program would last if those were bad, rather than good reports?

"We have had over 250,000 children in camp," he said. "We've been operating for 21 years. I'm going to knock on wood," he said, "but in all those 21 years we've never had a court action of any kind. Neither the Camp Commission nor any of the school districts has ever been sued for anything in its operation. And think of all the things that might happen. Transportation. Ragged terrain. Children living away from home. All such things."

I asked him whether there were any plans to put camps elsewhere in the county.

"We expect to need a fourth camp shortly, and there is a growing feeling that it would be good to have a camp in the desert and one on the seashore if possible. Oceanography is so important in San Diego, you know. We almost had a camp in the Borrego Desert, but at the time a strike broke out between the agricultural interests and the labor union, and we couldn't afford to get involved in that. I would like to see us first complete the building program, with the new bond issue, at Cuyamaca and Palomar, then develop the desert camp. I'd like to see this camp geared for those who are dropouts from school, and perhaps we could work out an arrangement with agriculture."

He looked for a minute at the edge of the woods. "Look right over that rock," he said. I looked, and then a patch of tan moved, and I saw the deer at the edge of the clearing.

"You know," he said, "we now are getting in camp the children of some of our first campers. And these parents come and tell us what they remember from their own camping experience. They mention all kinds of things. Food and hunger, some of them. Looking through the telescope. How they seined something out of the pond and looked at it beneath the microscope — maybe the first time they ever did that. Or seeing the beaver. Some of them will sing a camp song they probably haven't sung for a long, long time. Or they remember a tree they planted, and wonder if it is still there. These are memories that are warm and meaningful because they are part of a real wholesome experience.

"It goes back to the teacher," he said. "If it's a good teacher, who makes you feel secure and gives you the feeling that this is a wonderful subject you're exploring together. Each week the children are different, and each year some of the teachers are different, but this is the kind of experience we try to help them provide for the children."

I should have liked to spend more time at Camp Palomar, seen that meadow in the morning light, and perhaps gone on an observatory trip. But Camp Marston had a bed, and if I were there early enough in the morning I could see a variety of conservation experiences. So I left a group of Palomar campers looking with hand telescopes at some of the sky they had seen in the observatory photographs, and drove back over those mountain curves and switchbacks, thinking, as I drove, how fortunate San Diego had been to have leaders like Pumala and Fox in this program. It was dark now. When I got a long view I could see the lights of Escondido and Miramar bright and sharp against the blackness, and the lights of San Diego warm and soft under the night fog. I drove past the lake, over the plateau land, and back up the wooded slopes, and at Camp Marston they gave me a warm welcome and a cup of the coffee that never seems to keep one awake in the mountains. The beds were about the same as at Cuyamaca, and the temperature about the same, but that night it was my right foot that froze instead of my left.

# IX
# WHAT CONSERVATION MEANS

THE SCENE I REMEMBER BEST from Thursday morning at Marston was fourteen boys and girls standing in a recently burned area, looking closely for perhaps the first time at the grisly result of a forest fire. And a twelve-year-old girl looking around her with a stricken face, and saying, "It's like a cemetery!"

That gets ahead of the story. Breakfast at Marston was just as hearty as breakfast at Cuyamaca, and the campers did equal justice to it. Teachers reported on the previous night in the cabins. Only one of the cabins had had to be "entered," they said. The word "entered" was always said gravely, and had a special meaning at Marston. It meant that a teacher had to go into a cabin to quiet the campers so they could all go to sleep. All the other cabins had put themselves to bed, and there was praise for them. You could tell by the children's faces that this meant a great deal to them. For the one cabin that had been "entered," there would be a meeting after breakfast to talk about what had gone wrong there. A boy near me hung his head at this announcement. Somehow a deep pride in the responsible behavior of their cabins had been built into these children, and I made a note to ask Tom Brown how it was accomplished.

After breakfast, some children washed and dried the dishes

The scar left by a forest fire — "It's just like a cemetery!" one girl said.

and others cleaned the cabins, as at Cuyamaca, and then there was an activity meeting at which slides were shown of a recent fire in the forest nearby. Some of the pictures were quite spectacular: It must have been a bone-chilling experience to watch it coming. The pictures showed the first cloud of smoke, and the blaze at night, and carried the viewer through the next few days to the smoking corpses of trees after the fire had passed.

I tagged along after one of the conservation crews. A teacher named Fred was in charge, a quiet friendly fellow, comfortable to be around, who wore a red wool shirt and a grey hat, and had more grey in his hair than his age would justify. He strolled along with his little group, calling attention to this and that, and encouraging them to notice things and talk about them. They were standing in front of an outcropping of rock, when Fred said, "Listen carefully a minute." There was silence, and then he asked with a smile, "Did the rocks tell you anything?"

"No."

"Silly!" a girl said laughing.

"Of course, it's silly," said Fred. "The rocks don't *tell* you anything. The trees don't. How, then, do you learn something about them?"

"Look at them."

"Yes. You look very carefully."

"Pound them. Touch them. See how hard they are."

"Look them up in a book."

"Yes. But the most important thing is to look very carefully. The scientist observes very closely. This is what we have to do."

Walking along, he asked them what they would expect to see along this woodsy path that they might be interested in. They mentioned animals — rabbits, birds, a raccoon. Would you expect to see a raccoon now, he asked. No, they decided; Mr. Raccoon would probably be out at night. How could you tell he had been around, then, asked Fred. They talked about this and other things as they walked. One boy spotted a huge nest in a tree, and they discussed what had lived in it. Another boy found the beginning of a woodrat's nest. It seemed to me they had become quite alert to the natural environment around them. And then they were out of the woods into the scar left on the rolling hillsides by the forest fire.

It took a little while for the sight to sink into them. They looked around at the charred stalks of manzanita protruding only a few inches out of the ground, the black dead pine trunks, the bare brown soil, and a pile of fireplace brick and foundation stones that had been a mountain house. One girl found a piece of burned bone, and they talked a minute about how they could be sure it was bone, and what kind of animal might have died in the fire.

Then Fred said, "Stop a minute and look around you. Look all around you. How do you feel about this place?"

That was when it hit them. The little girl with the stricken face said, "It's just like a cemetery."

"It's awful," said another girl.

"Like dead things all around you," said a boy.

They were obviously moved.

"Look how beautiful that ridge is over there," said a boy whose sweatshirt read "Giants."

"Yes, the fire didn't reach there," said Fred. "What kind of forest was it, before the fire?"

"Manzanita."

"Yes, mostly manzanita."

"Oak?"

"Has anyone seen signs of an oak?"

"Pine."

"Yes, lots of pine."

It was hot under heavy jackets. We took off our wraps and stopped for a drink. Marston style was like Cuyamaca style: poured into one's mouth from six inches above.

We sat down and talked a minute about how this fire probably started, and then Bob asked what had happened to our hillside as a result of the fire.

"The hillside is bare," a boy said.

"There's erosion."

"What's bad about erosion?" asked Fred.

"Soil is washed away. The trees won't grow."

"Anything else?"

"It's ugly!"

"Yes, it is ugly, isn't it?"

Fred asked whether this erosion would have any effect on San Diego.

"We can't come out here to see these woods."

"Yes," said Fred. "Anything else? Where do you think the soil that washes off will go to?"

"It'll wash down."

"Will it wash down to the bottom of the gully and stop?"

"No."

"Lots of it will stop, but where will the rest of it go?"

"It'll go down there" — gesturing toward the west.

"Down there, and farther and farther . . ."

"If you could trace a few drops of the soil, where might you follow it?"

"To a farm."

"Would it be good or bad for the farm?"

They decided it would be partly good, partly bad. It might leave the farm some new soil, but also might wash away some of the farm and cover up fields with mud.

"Can you think of a way it might affect us in San Diego directly?" asked Fred.

It might pollute the drinking water; it might stop up the pipes and the reservoirs.

"What could we do to help here?" Fred asked.

The suggestions came from all over the group: Plant trees. Get the manzanita growing again. Build rock dams. Pile some rocks to keep the soil from washing away. Dig drainage ditches.

"Wait a minute," said Fred. "Wait a minute. Maybe we're going too fast. Is there really a problem right here? Look around hard. If there isn't a problem, why work here? If there *is* a problem, exactly what is it?"

That set them looking around again. They walked around and peered closely at the ground and talked about what they found. There were plentiful signs of erosion.

"Where do you see the signs of erosion?" asked Fred.

They pointed to some of it.

"Now what's the difference between the places where you do see erosion, and where you don't?"

The erosion, they found, occurred mostly in the open, where there were no rocks or growing things, and where there was nothing to stop the flow of the water.

"Look at the ground around these rocks," said Fred, and they gathered around him to look at it. "Do you see much erosion around where the rocks are? Look at it hard."

They said that around the rocks there were no signs of the soil washing away.

"So you see," said Fred, "where there are no rocks or just loose soil that might wash away. But each rock acts like a little dam, and keeps the water from washing away the soil. So what might we do to check erosion?"

"Put rocks on the ground."

"Right. We could either build a dam or put rocks on the ground. Remember that sometimes we can look around and see what nature has done, and get some idea what it is that we need to do. We can look at where there has been erosion, and figure out how best to counteract it. How can we decide that?"

". . . Look?"

"Yes, look at it closely, and see what the problem is, and what nature has done that might give us an idea what to do."

"But where would we get rocks to use here?" Fred asked. They laughed a little, with him, because there was no shortage of rocks on that hillside. "Would it be a good idea to move a rock like this over to this bare place?"

They saw quickly that it would do no good to leave one part of the hillside without protection, in order to protect another. So they would carry rocks from one of the numerous piles. They began happily to plan what kind of erosion control they would use.

"Maybe you can think of a way to do this that no other campers have thought of," Fred said to them.

"Would you like to work with a partner today?" he was suggesting as I left, and it occurred to me how seldom these children were directly ordered to do something.

I walked over to a nearby hillside where a conservation crew was about to cut down a pine tree. This was also in the burned area. The tree was charred and dead, and by the time I got there they had already discussed the danger of this tree becoming infested by beetles and the need to remove it before that happened. George, the captain of the desert rim trip, was the teacher in charge. He waved at me and told me to sit down in the circle of sixth graders who were discussing the problem of tree-felling.

"Now, what do we have to think about when we decide to cut a tree?" he was asking.

"Whether it's dead?"

"Yes, that's one thing. What next?"

"Well, if we're going to take one down, we ought to be sure it won't hit another one."

"OK. We have to think about it in relation to other trees. That's good. What else?"

"Where we want it to fall?"

"What's going to determine what direction the tree is going to fall?" asked George.

"Wind?"

"If the wind is blowing, that's important, isn't it?"

"Yes."

"Do all trees grow straight up?"

"No," they said.

"Is this tree growing straight up?"

"Yes."

"No, not quite."

"Almost."

"Well, it looks pretty straight from this side, but what if we

"We have to cut it down to kill the beetles."

walked around to the other side?"

They talked it over. The tree was on a hillside, and they thought the angles might fool them. George asked how they could decide for sure whether it was straight or not. They didn't come up with a very good idea, and so he said:

"How many have ever heard of a plumb bob?"

"A what?"

"A plumb bob. Remember a surveyor, one of those men that look through a little telescope when they are surveying land, and they have a little string hanging down with a metal ball at the end of it. That's called a plumb bob. How many have ever seen one of these?"

They seemed not to have come into contact with that device.

"You see why they use it, don't you? They are trying to get an absolutely straight line, and so they have to find out what direction is straight up and down. So they hang that little ball on the string. We could use that method, couldn't we? Has anybody got a string?"

Nobody had.

"Well, we could use a shoestring," said George, "but let's use the axe. If the axe hangs down without anything pulling it one direction or the other, it ought to hang straight down, oughtn't it? Do you think I could line that up with the tree, and see if it is growing absolutely straight?"

They sighted along the axe.

"If I looked at the tree just from this side, could I find out all

I need to know?" asked George.

"You should look at the other side, too."

"It could be leaning one way but not the other."

"All right," said George, and moved to the other side. "Take a look," he said. "Would you say the tree might be leaning at an angle now?"

Yes, they said.

"Which way?"

*That* way.

"OK, the tree is leaning that way. That might give me an idea how it will fall. Is there anything else that might give me an idea?"

Limbing and bucking the tree.

They talked that over. Would the incline of the hill have an effect? Would the tree be more likely to fall downhill? George told them to look at a small tree nearby and tell him whether anything on that tree might determine which way it fell. They saw at once that most of the branches were on one side. The branches on the tree they were planning to cut were fairly even, but somewhat heavier on the downhill side. George raised the question of whether all trees were round, and if not, why not. After they decided that not all trees were round, someone suggested that maybe the bark looked round but the tree inside wasn't. George trimmed off a band of bark so they could see the main part of the tree. After a while, he summed up the evidence: It looked as though the tree would be more likely to fall downhill.

Is that the way we *want* it to fall?" he asked.

And when they said that was the desired direction, he challenged them, "Why?"

"Is there anything *we* can do," he asked, after they had advanced some ideas on that question, "is there anything we ourselves can do to control the direction of fall?"

"Well, you could just cut it until it was, well, most of the way through, and then people could get and push one way, and, well, then you could saw the rest of the way through, and then keep pushing, and, well, it should fall *that* way." The boy looked as though he wanted to get his hands on the axe and demonstrate.

"OK," said George. "That could be one way. Charlie?"

"You could take a chip out of the front," said Charlie, "and then go around to the other side of it, you know, to the back of it, and then cut it and it should fall down."

"What would taking that chip out do?" asked George.

"Then it wouldn't have to go over that much. It would weaken it on that side."

"That's good thinking," said George. "If we cut in like this, and cut a section out of the tree and weaken it, and cut that section facing the direction we want it to fall, and then start cutting from the back, a little higher up, the tree would probably fall in that direction. Do you agree?"

And so gradually they worked their way up to the moment of putting tool to tree. They had a two-man crosscut saw, and a number of smaller bow saws which were to be used for trimming the branches and cutting smaller parts of the tree after it was down, and an axe which, George made clear, was to be used only by the teachers.

"How many trees are we going to cut down?" asked a very blackhaired boy.

"This morning I hope we get *one* cut down," said George.

That little conversation turned out to be more significant than it sounded, for when they had checked out the proper ways of using the tools, and chosen the first pair of children to use the crosscut saw, and begun the undercut, the tree declined to cooperate. When a ponderosa pine, like the one they were working on, is burned, the sap must harden and become gum-like. The saw would bite in an inch or two, and stick. George would put in some lubricant — I didn't know whether it was oil or thinner — and the saw would move for a little while, and stick again.

Another pair of sawyers replaced the first two. And still the cut moved very slowly. I could see it was going to be a long war, and was rather glad when Tom appeared and offered to take me to see some of the conservation projects that had already been done.

I confess I was astonished by what he showed me. I had been concentrating on one tree and the beginning of one rock apron, and now I was seeing the result of some years of conservation activity by thousands of sixth graders. Here was a whole mountain meadow full of rock aprons and rock dams, obviously reclaimed from bare eroded soil to a luxurious growth of grass. Here was a channel where the water seemed to run off after storms: Undercuts had been smoothed out so grass could grow again and hold the banks, and dams put in to slow up the flow. Here was a piece of forest so beautifully cleaned out that it made one think of the park-like forests of Germany. I was impressed by the amount of hard physical work this obviously represented, and asked Tom whether the children resented having to work so hard.

"Quite the contrary," he said. "It means a great deal to them. They come to feel strongly about fire and erosion and destruction of the forest, and want to do something about it." I mentioned the little scene I had observed this morning when the children

Soil erosion control — building rock aprons and check dams.

came first into the burned area. He nodded. "Yes, we see this again and again. They feel it very much. After they have been here a little while. Then the natural environment begins to mean more to them than it did before. Object to working on it? Heavens, no! This is one place where they can see a result of what they do. It's one of the things they most often mention later, and some of them have come back to see how 'their' conservation area looks now."

The rolling meadow land around Camp Marston is not a state park, Tom explained. Most of it is privately owned. Therefore, there are no restrictions on collecting, and the only restrictions on conservation work are those decided on with the owners of the land. We looked at some beautiful country in the course of our little hike. There was one grassy meadow that sloped down to a pond, rimmed by trees. The scene was so European that I almost expected to find a chateau or an English country house beside the water.

At lunch I asked a boy who had been pulling the crosscut saw whether they had got the tree down. "Not quite," he said. "We asked to go back this afternoon and finish it."

After lunch I asked Tom to answer some questions for me before I departed for Cuyamaca about how Camp Marston achieved the pride and responsibility that its campers seem to feel in their cabin behavior. I said to Tom that if I recalled right, all except one cabin had put themselves to bed last night with little need for supervision or intervention by the teacher in charge. That seemed to be quite an accomplishment for 12-year-olds away from home for a week in the mountains, and I wondered how it was brought about.

He said they felt that what they do with cabin living is one of the most important aspects of the program. Fred, the teacher whom I had followed on conservation that morning, came over to sit with us, and Tom suggested that he tell me exactly how the teachers handle this matter.

"We do feel it's probably the strongest thing we have to offer," Fred said, "this democratic procedure. And the thing is that it really happens here. It really does work!

"Unless you're here for the entire week, it's sometimes rather difficult to see exactly what takes place. But let's begin with Monday. One of the first things the kids do is to sit down and try to look ahead. They make their own rules for the cabins."

"Just as you probably saw at Cuyamaca," Tom interjected. "What do you really try to do with an orientation, Fred? I think this is the key to it. What is your purpose in guiding the youngsters through this orientation? Is it to solve all the problems of the week?"

"Oh, no," said Fred. "Perhaps it doesn't even make a lot of sense to many of the kids, at the beginning, but it's only a short time until a problem does develop, and then we can throw the problem back at the kids. They have made the rules, and they have to carry the ball. The problem of being noisy or roughhousing at night, we've discussed this, and they have a general idea what they ought and ought not to be doing, and how to take care of their own situation."

"Is the teacher in the cabin at all with them the first night?" I asked.

"The number of teachers on night duty depends on the size of the group," explained Tom. "With small groups there are two; with large groups, four teachers will sleep with the children in the cabins."

"The teachers don't go to bed until after the kids are in bed and quiet," said Fred. "Once the teachers go to bed, they are in a cabin, but until 10:30 or 11:00 they are outside moving from cabin to cabin.

"That first night we give them a good orientation before they come over for bed. There's a story at night, for one thing. It sets the tone, and gives us a chance to talk with the kids about what is expected. And of course, even so we still have, and expect, our problems.

"We usually have problems on Monday, but this gives us something to work with the rest of the week. They'll be talking on Monday night. We usually have to enter each cabin at least once. And when we do we talk about this: 'Listen, fellows, you told us what you were going to do in these cabins. What happened?' It's not a scolding; It's not a shouting match. Usually just a very gentle talk."

"We're realistic and we're honest," said Tom. "Monday night we expect it's going to be noisy up there, as Fred said. Because these are children, and they have problems. Our orientation is nothing more than setting a base from which we can work as the week goes along. They sometimes don't even realize the problems when they are going through the orientation. They have to live this first night to find out what some of their problems are. We don't expect them to be perfect. But once they experience some of these problems, the following day there's a better chance of working with that group.

"It would be very easy," he said, "to come in here and say: 'Now, you kids are going to do this, this, this, and this!' That is the easy way. At the cabin meetings we had, this morning and yesterday morning, for the ones which had behavior problems the night before — at those meetings the youngsters came back to the cabins expecting to be scolded. Uh-uh! Nothing like it. We come back to the cabin with them: 'All right, fellows, we had some problems here last night. What were our problems, and what are we going to do about them?' We may or may not solve the problems at that meeting, but we're trying to let these youngsters honestly have a chance at solving their own problems.

"We don't even expect a perfect night Tuesday night. But they have the chance. Tuesday night we can expect a great deal more. The youngsters have a better idea of what they can work for. And so they work and they improve. Cabin clean-up enters into their problems and planning. We try to help them build pride in the place where they live. Fred, what were you going to say?"

"By Wednesday night, at least," said Fred. "The kids can see the progress they've made. In fact, it has such an effect that when one or two boys might be detracting from the cabin record, *we* don't have to take care of it. They talk to those one or two boys themselves and let them know that they are disappointed in what they are doing. So as pride develops, they more and more take care of their own problems."

"A great majority do a very fine job, even on Tuesday night," said Tom. "There isn't any set time when we can expect the cabin to square around. Some groups—depending on their backgrounds, maybe—may not achieve until Thursday, or even Friday morning. So we don't set any particular goal; we just keep aware of the progress they're making, and try to encourage it."

Fred was called away, and Tom carried on alone.

"When we try to build pride in them," he said, "we always work in as positive a way as possible. Always stating things positively, rather than negatively. We report honestly in the mornings, and call a spade a spade, but we let these kids know that we *want* them to have success. They meet friendship from their teachers, rather than scoldings.

"Did you see their faces this morning?" he asked. "Those whose cabins got good reports? Did you see how wonderfully proud they were?"

I asked him how he came into the program. He said he was born in Warren, Ohio, and came out to college at San Diego State. At that time he hardly knew there was a back country in San Diego County, and wouldn't be caught dead in it, anyway. Mountains weren't his cup of tea. And then he heard of an opportunity to observe a different kind of program in education, and in his senior year came to Camp Palomar for a week as an educational cadet. What he saw in that one week, pretty well convinced him that this was something he would like to do. When he graduated in midyear he got a telephone call from Denver Fox, and went to work in the program, expecting to stay a year. After 17 years he is still there.

I mentioned how pleased I was with the teaching I had observed, and with the quality and personalities of his young teachers. "The staff feels as much pride in this thing as the children do," he said. "We feel the same wonderful sense of pride as we see the cabins achieve, achieve, and achieve, and when Friday comes if we know we've done a good job we're happy, and when we haven't we're pretty honest about it and pretty dissatisfied. We critique every week. We meet together on Friday after the last bus has pulled out, usually out there on that log, and the first question they ask me is, "Tom, did we win?"

I asked him whether he didn't have a number of visitors thinking of starting outdoor education programs (he nodded his head) and what kind of advice he gave them.

"I tell them to try to get the program started *right*," he said. "It doesn't have to start big, if it starts right. Usually the first question I ask them is what kind of staffing are they going to have? Are they going to start on a shoestring and hope they'll get better later? Have they seen enough programs to know what kind of experiences they want to offer their children? Are they going to be able to make their program an integral part of the school, so that it becomes something very vital, and when the school district looks around for something to cut they don't think of outdoor education first?

"I've heard Denver say many times," he said, "that we are only one third of the process here. The classroom teacher has two thirds of it — the preparation and the follow-up. That classroom teacher may spend five, six, seven weeks getting the class in a frame of mind so that they can learn the most in camp. So we can't claim all the credit. It's a cooperative thing. We're still very much a part of those classrooms 57 miles away. And that is part of what I am talking about when I say that the outdoor education program should be tightly bound into the school program.

"But in the final analysis, we're on the firing line right here," he said. "The ones who ultimately make or break the program are right here. I can think of so many hundreds of fine people who have worked in our program in these camps, and made contributions that helped build excellence into it — right here in these camps. I am confident that it is the quality of this program that has saved it and kept it alive through these years, and that is why I

The classroom teacher plans with the children for a good week in the outdoors.

always ask the people who come to me about a program—usually before anything else, I ask them, what kind of staff are you going to have?"

I said goodbye to Tom and drove back through Julian toward Cuyamaca. At one place, as I drove out of the camp, I could see Mount Palomar to the north and the lineup of three peaks—North, Middle, and Cuyamaca—to the southwest. On the side of Palomar and the eastern slope of Cuyamaca, as here at Marston, little groups of sixth graders would at that moment be heading out into the woods, perhaps to cut down a stubborn tree, or find an ancient Indian village, or look at the great nebula of Andromeda. When I came to the desert vista on the road south from Julian, I parked the car for a moment and had a long look over that 50-million-year-old sea bed, and the line of blue that was the Salton Sea just over the second range of lavender mountains. I took some pleasure in believing that, at the very moment, 15 or 20 sixth graders would probably be on the desert rim, looking at that same view, and fingering pieces of sandstone or schist. And before the afternoon was over, they would be able to look around them and think: Old Desert, I know what lies down there for a mile or so below your sand and cactus, and how it got there. Old Mountain, I know how you got here, and how these rocks got piled up as they are, and where they came from. And Old Earth, I own a little key now that will help unlock some of your secrets.

# X
## THE LABORATORIES OF NATURE

WHEN I CAME TO THE ROAD that turned off toward Middle Peak, there was Camp Cuyamaca's yellow school bus. Ernie was opening the gate to a private road that led into the woods. I pulled up alongside the bus, hands began to wave at the windows, and the boy with the Yankees jacket called out the open front door: "Where have you *been*?"

Ernie told me to park my car and ride along with them for a few minutes. They were going to take a side trip on their way to a conservation site. It would be something I would like to see.

Inside the bus every seat was full except one for me, and two on the back bench. Ernie was driving. Dottie had propped herself up in front like a tour guide. All the boys and girls wore high galoshes, apparently from the camp supply: They were expecting wet grass or snow. Little George had found a pair of galoshes that looked big enough for both him and the boy who sat beside him. This was like old home week — so many of the children I had come to know. Little Cindy from La Mesa, who had enlisted me to make "hills" for her on the Monkey Bridge. Tough Dan, John the lanky boy who lived with his aunt. There was a slow-spoken boy who had been with us on the hike on Tuesday morning, and several of the youngsters whose faces I had come to know in activities or at table. I couldn't remember all their names, but was astonished to find out how many I could identify by an experience, a way of dressing, or a characteristic behavior.

"What's been happening?" I asked, like any other returning traveler, anxious for news from home.

Weather had got steadily better since Tuesday night, they said. They had stayed in camp Wednesday, but today hikes were on. Everybody, or almost everybody, had gone on a half-day hike today. These particular youngsters had their hikes in the forenoon, and they were full of accounts of arrow-makers' villages, and climbing the mesa. There was a place called Rock Canyon, they said, where a gigantic yucca was in bloom, where the rock walls were fifty feet high, and a waterfall tumbled down like a toy Yosemite. Their really startling news was that Northwind had got the second highest rating that morning on cabin cleanup. One of the girls' cabins had won, of course, but this was the first time one of the boys' cabins had come in ahead of a girls' cabin. "Was it a big score?" I asked. "I think Northwind got 10.4, and Eastwind

123

9.5. That's about two touchdowns—or one unmade bed," said Dottie. I looked around at the Northwind boys on the bus. Even Dan looked pleased.

Dottie told us that we were going up Middle Peak. We were on a narrow woods road, unpaved except for a little gravel. It curved upward through pine, oak, and birch woods. Occasionally we got a vista through the trees, and could see that we were far above the valley and the reservoir. Once the bus stuck in ruts, and everybody piled out. We gave hand signals, and Ernie went back and forth until the bus was on flat ground again. A quarter of a mile farther, the road ended in front of a rustic hunting cabin high on the mountain side.

Dottie said that the owner of this land used to come up in summer and hunting season, and loved it so much he didn't want anything changed. So when he died they still kept it as it was, and it looks exactly as it did many years ago.

Even the noisiest children were quiet as they took in the scene. We stood in aisles of enormous trees — not as spectacular as the coast redwoods, but much higher than the growth at Cuyamaca. The sun filtered down through the branches and mottled the green carpet. As long as we were quiet we could hear the wind moving through the valley, rustling the trees below us. When we walked over to the edge of the shelf where the road ended, it seemed as though all San Diego County was stretched out before us. From almost above it, we could see the lake and what had been the gold mine. Looking along the range we could see nearly as far as Palomar; in fact, one boy said he thought he could make out one of the white domes of the observatory. I thought I recognized the wooded valley where Camp Marston would be, but couldn't make out the buildings.

"Over this way's the desert," said Ernie. "Over this way, the valley and San Diego. If your arm is long enough you can *touch* the Indian reservation down there."

"When are we going up the mountain?" asked one lad in a droll way. Ernie looked at him in amazement, and then chuckled. It reminded me of Richard Halliburton, when he had climbed the Matterhorn, recording in his diary that at last he could spit a mile.

For the most part we didn't talk, just looked. And then turned to the snow bank. There had been snow at numerous places along the road on the way up, but here was a bank of it, perhaps two or three feet deep. Some of the boys looked questions at the teachers.

"I don't see why you shouldn't throw a few snowballs," said Dottie.

The air was soon full of them. I wound up and pitched the first fast ball I had thrown for 15 years. It was a perfect strike against a stump that fortunately was not holding a bat. The pitch would have done credit to Bob Feller. The only trouble was that I felt as though I had thrown my shoulder and half my back muscles along with the ball. I retired from baseball and followed Ernie along a trail where he said he wanted to show us something.

What he showed us was the largest sugar pine tree I had ever seen. "How old would it be?" Dan asked him. "At least a thousand years," he said. "If we cut it down, we could tell from tree rings, but this is one of the things the owner said should never be touched. And I suppose it never will be, even though it's dead."

The giant sugar pine — "I feel like I'm pressing against a thousand years!"

"See how many of you it takes to circle the tree," suggested Dottie. Some of them joined hands, and I think it took nine children, arms extended, to reach around the gigantic trunk. Some of the children cocked their heads far back and looked up along the trunk of the tree to its majestic crown against the blue sky. Many of them went up to press against the rough old bark, or leaned against the huge trunk. Looking at their faces, I realized that these children were having an experience. This was a "happening." They were making personal contact with something that had lived a thousand years. It was a metaphor of man's yearning to possess his own past and know his inheritance. There were no wisecracks, now, no horseplay. These children, whether they could have put words to it or not, were deeply impressed, and some of them, as I could see from their faces, were thinking long thoughts.

We took a farewell look at the great tree, climbed back on the bus, and coasted down the mountain to a sunny grove, to unload children and Swedish bow saws and canteens. Ernie took me the rest of the way down to the gate, and I drove on to Cuyamaca.

The children and teachers were not the same ones; the scenery and buildings were different; and yet I had an odd sensation, as I returned to Cuyamaca that I had never left—I had merely stepped around the corner to another part of the same camp. The program, the approach, the type of teachers and children, were so similar that one could step from Palomar to Marston to Cuyamaca with no sharp sense of change. Around the quadrangle of Cuyamaca a number of activities were in progress. Though nearly half the children were on afternoon hikes, and a bus load were on conservation, 60 or 70 were still left in camp. I looked in on pond biology, where Marty was preparing 15 boys and girls to go forth with seines and pans to the pond. They had apparently been talking about the meaning of biology, the nature of living things, and the importance of chlorophyl and such things, and were now centering on ponds.

"How would you tell someone what a pond is?" Marty was asking.

"It's closed. It's water, of course."

"It's small."

"Smaller than what?" challenged Marty.

"A lake. An ocean."

"What else can we say about a pond?"

"It's *still* water. It doesn't flow."

Marty asked them to name some bodies of flowing water, and they suggested rivers, creeks, canals, waterfalls.

"Is a pond deep?"

"No, shallow."

"How shallow?"

"A few feet?"

"Good," said Marty. "So a pond is small, still, shallow, and closed. Now what would you expect to find in a pond, besides water?"

"Plants?"

"Where would you expect to find them in the pond?"

They decided plants would most likely be in the shallow parts.

"Why?" That question kept coming back.

They talked it over, and decided plants would grow where they could get light.

"Why is that important to them?"

That brought them back to chlorophyl and photosynthesis.

Marty drew a big picture of a pond, and they began to populate it with living things.

"Do all plants have roots in the ground?"

They thought plants did, but Marty walked over to one of the aquariums and showed them a floating plant.

"Will there be any animals in the pond?"

"Oh, yes."

"What kind?"

"Fish."

"Frogs."

"Tadpoles."

"Lizards."

"Are plants important in any way to the pond animals?"

"Yes. They eat them."

"Right. Any other reason why they are important?"

"Make clothes of them?"

"The pond animals do?"

"No, we do."

"All right, what do the pond animals use plants for, besides food?"

A girl in orange trousers suggested they furnished protection, and Marty drew out the idea that animals can hide and live amidst the plants.

Studying life in the pond.

Collecting specimens for further study in the biology lab — "Something that must have been for most of the children simply a spot of muddy water was turning into a very active community of living things."

A girl with a green sweater raised her hand, and subsided with embarrassment when Marty called on her. She had forgotten the question.

"Would you expect to find birds around the pond?"

"Oh, yes."

"Why?"

"They feed on insects?" asked a boy with a Scottish beanie.

"Then there must be insects in the pond. What kind of insects?"

They talked about insects for a while, and Marty got out some large pictures on the kinds of insects they might see at the pond. "Can you tell me an insect that lays its eggs on the water?" she asked.

The girl in the orange trousers said that she thought the mosquito did that. Marty showed her a picture of the mosquito larvae and pointed out that the little creatures had snorkels. "When we put oil on a pond to control mosquitoes it generally kills the eggs, and then takes care of the larvae by filling up their snorkels," she explained. "Of course, it probably kills everything else in the pond, too," she added.

What was happening in that class, I saw, was that something that must have been for most of the children simply a spot of muddy water was turning into a very active community of living things, dependent in different ways on each other, being born, living, eating, being eaten, fleeing, pursuing, some of them changing in form throughout life, and dying. None of these children would ever again think of a pond as simply water.

"Now, let's go down to the pond," said Marty. She told them to divide into teams of three. Each team had a seine and some pans. Marty advised them to look at the pond for a little while and see what they could tell about it without touching it, then choose a station and find out what they could about what was in the pond— on the surface, along the edge, in the deeper parts, among the plants. When they seined out something that they thought was interesting they could put it in water in their pans, and save it to show to the others. After a little while, she said, we'll all get to-

Carving and shaping alabaster.

gether again, and talk about what we have discovered about the pond.

They trooped happily down to the water. I looked in on Roy's geology group.

They were poring over a line of rocks of many different kinds. He had apparently challenged them to tell what they could about the history of the rocks simply by looking at them and handling them.

Two boys were puzzling over a large piece of reddish black lava. "Will you hoist this once?" sweatshirt asked sportshirt. Sportshirt picked it up. "It's as light as a feather," he said. Roy came over, and the whole group gathered around to marvel at the rock. "Why should it be so light?" asked Roy. They talked about it: Maybe it had air bubbles in it. "Is there anything you can see about it to tell you whether there might be air bubbles?" asked Roy. They decided it might have bubbled out of a volcano. And why would it bubble out? And where had it come from? And so back to the molten core of the earth.

After they had talked about a piece of sedimentary rock, and traced it, as the boys and girls had done on the desert rim, back to some ancient hillside and stream, Roy said he was going to take them on a little walk around the edge of camp. He wanted them to keep their eyes open for "soil factories," where rocks were being decomposed into soil to start over again the long process they had been talking about—from rocks to soil to sediment to sedimentary rock. So they went happily and found lichen, and rocks that were cracking from roots and ice, and streams washing against rocks, and so forth.

Down at the pond, the young biologists were happily sharing their discoveries. When I found them, they were discussing algae, what it was and what its uses were. They had some specimens that Marty thought might be worth looking at more closely, and she asked whether they would like to see them under the bioscope. So they trooped up the hill again, balancing their pans carefully to keep from spilling the water.

I looked into the room where Walt had been explaining telescopes to a small group. Camp Cuyamaca owned several small telescopes, including a very fine Questar. Looking at them wasn't quite like visiting the 200-inch telescope at Mt. Palomar, but at least the children could see the difference between reflecting and refracting instruments, and on clear evenings they could look at planets and galaxies.

Walt obviously had a slower group than either of the two I had seen in action that morning. There were fewer questions and answers, fewer individual excursions into learning, longer periods of explanation and lecturing. When I came in, Walt was trying to convey some information about the nature of light.

"Why do we see lightning before we hear thunder?" he asked.

"Clouds get in the way," said a boy.

"The sound barrier," suggested a second lad.

A brown-skinned girl said quite precisely that light goes 186,000 miles a second, and sound goes a lot slower.

Walt seemed to cheer up. "Very good," he said. "Now let's suppose that sound goes about one fifth of a mile a second, and light goes so fast that for all practical purposes we can forget the time that it takes to move a few miles. Now suppose it takes five seconds after you see the flash of lightning before you hear the thunder; how far is the lightning away from you?"

It puzzled them. I don't know why. It took a couple of minutes before they figured out that the lightning must have been about a mile away.

Walt tried to get over to them the idea of wave motion, and of the great distance a light year stands for, but the class was not very responsive, and so he turned to simpler things, with which both he as an experienced woodsman and his pupils seemed more at home.

"Anybody know how a sundial works?"

When they proved they did, he told them the old woodsman's trick of using a watch as a sundial to tell directions. Sight over the hour hand toward the sun, he said. Don't look right at the sun; make the shadow fall along the hour hand. Then halfway between the hour hand and 12 o'clock will be south.

They marveled a little at that and a few of them began to experiment with their watches. "For instance," Walt said, "if it's ten o'clock, and you point the hour hand at the sun, south will be right over 11 o'clock. What if you would take your watch outside now, could you find south?"

Sure, they all said.

"How?" asked Walt.

"Just point the hour hand at the sun."

"Could you tell where the sun is right now?"

They looked outside. Clouds had come in and were covering up the sun. "Maybe not," they said.

"Maybe not," said Walt. "Might be too cloudy."

He looked at his own watch.

"What *could* you find out if you took your watch outside and looked at it now?" he asked.

Don't know, they said.

"That it's time you're back in the cabin for showers!" said Walt, with a twinkle.

# XI
## LAST EVENING IN CAMP

"HOW HAVE MY LITTLE FRIENDS from Northwind been doing while I was gone?" I asked Harry before dinner.

"I *thought* you had adopted that cabin," he said "They've been doing much better. They seem to be coming around. Roy, you were down there last night. How was the cabin?"

"They behaved very well," said Roy. "No special trouble. And they had a good clean cabin this morning. That cabin has some real problems, but it seems they're solving most of them."

"What's Dan been doing?" I asked.

"No more trouble from him," said Harry. "He's not a very outgoing boy, but no more performances like that one on Tuesday."

"I saw him on conservation today," I said. "On Middle Peak."

"You know that boy David," said Roy. "I had him on a hike this morning and kept my fingers crossed. But I couldn't have been more surprised. He was about the best observer I had. And when we sat down to listen to the forest, and a couple of kids didn't quiet down so we could hear, David just took them apart."

"Took them apart?" I asked.

"Just said something to them. I didn't hear exactly what he said. But they certainly shut up."

Thursday was the big evening in camp. There would be a candlelight ceremony at dinner. Then each of the cabins would sing a song, which, I was informed, had been surreptitiously practiced during the last day or so. And finally each cabin would hold its own meeting and try to sum up the week.

At dinner I sat among old friends. Across the table was little George and the boy with the Yankees jacket, and Maria, the dark pretty Spanish girl. Next to me was Miss I. Magnin — Sally — in her sleek blue sweater, and beyond her a diffident boy who had given some of the best answers in geology that afternoon.

"What do you think of these science classes up here?" I asked him.

"Like them," he said. "Wish we had them a few days longer."

"How are they different from classes you have at school?" I asked.

They talked that over among themselves, and the boy said in his slow, careful way: "There isn't so much difference, and yet there is too. Up here they don't spend so much time getting you to remember things: They try to get you to *see* things."

"Wonder how he lives."

"Yeah," said George.

"In San Diego it would be like the teacher walking down the street with you and saying all the time: Now what do you think is going on here? Or why does this look this way?" said the slow-spoken boy.

"You know," said Sally, "what really bowls you over is that they expect *you* to go out and find out all about rocks or ponds or something. And then you find you CAN!"

"Well, at least we can tell *something* about it," said the slow-voiced boy.

"All right," said the sweater girl, a little irritated. "But you know I never thought about it that way before. I never thought of figuring out some of these questions without a science book or an encyclopedia. Pond biology today was real fun!"

"I didn't see you in that class," I said to her.

"I was being hard to see," she dimpled. "I was afraid Marty would ask me a question."

The slow-spoken boy was named Harold. He said his father worked on the new stadium in San Diego, where the Chargers would play football. Did he have any science hobbies? Not yet, but thought he'd begin a rock collection. What did he want to be when he grew up? He didn't know — maybe a teacher, maybe an engineer. "Maybe a Hippie," said the sweater girl. "Not him," said Maria, her eyes at half mast.

Candles were on the tables. After the usual enormous dinner the lights were doused, matches flared, and the dining room exchanged its institutional look for the warm and intimate tones of candlelight. Sharp corners disappeared. The signs that kept the system moving — "Porky," "Smokey," "In-Skunk," "Out-Skunk," "Plates," and so forth — faded into the shadows. The two girls beside me became excited eyes and white foreheads framed in dark hair.

Harry made the little talk that goes with candlelight ceremonies everywhere: A little candle shines a long way. It stands for the human spirit — pride, dignity, love. It stands for the spirit of Cuyamaca. We soon lose our little glow if we forget. If we remember, we can make the world a better place.

Sentimental, yes; but friendly and personal to the situation.

Then the cabin groups came up one by one to the front of the room to sing. Carla's Westwind came first. They stood in front of the fireplace, in front of the Porky and Smokey barrels. A little girl stepped forward and announced they were going to sing "Today." Perhaps it was a tribute to the candlelight that there were no wisecracks about that.

Carla was the best musician among the counselors. She played the piano and the guitar, and kept a volume of Bach on the old upright in the staff lounge, but her little singers did not do her justice. They sang in sweet, trembly girlish voices, but were horribly self-conscious, got a little off key, and almost forgot the last verse. They hurried back to their seats when the applause came. "Poor lambs! Scared stiff," whispered Carla, when she came back to my table.

Then came Southwind, Don's group. A little fellow stood in front of the group. "Ten-shun!" he said, and they straightened up in something approximating a military manner. "For your pleasure," the young commander said to us, "we are going to sing 'The Marines' Hymn'." They sang it with great vigor, and drew mighty applause. They about-faced smartly and marched back to their seats. It would have been even more impressive if the last boy had not swung out a little too far and knocked over the Smokey garbage can.

Edna's Eastwind cabin put on the smoothest show. They sang a medley beginning with something like "L-O-double-L-Y P-O-P spells lolly pop" — in two harmonizing parts, no less. They were very good, and during the applause someone called "Again!" Edna and Carla stood in front of their girls and directed. The male teachers, on the other hand, merely called their boys forward, and then left them on their own.

Ernie called the Northwind boys forward. I didn't expect much from them, and couldn't have been more surprised. When Ernie sat down, a young fellow with a pink and white shirt came out in front to beat time, and still another boy appeared with a guitar to play the accompaniment. They sang "Blowin' in the Wind." The voices were embryo baritones mixed with boy sopranos, and it wasn't as smooth as Eastwind; but the guitarist added something, and the boys obviously enjoyed the song. When they came to the third verse, some of the girls around the room were singing softly along with them. We enjoyed Northwind most, perhaps because we hadn't expected much. Eastwind was the most polished, but Northwind was the most fun.

"Ernie, I didn't know you had this talent," Carla said to him afterward.

"I don't," said Ernie. "These little characters took over. They taught *me* the song."

A little later the cabins convened their meetings. The meetings all came at the same time, and I had to choose one. Not unexpectedly, I chose to hear Northwind. If there were any fireworks, they would probably come out of that meeting. And besides I wanted to see what those boys I had come to know best would have to say about camp.

They were seated on the floor, in a circle, in the center of the cabin, with three candles furnishing the only light. I crept in as quietly as possible and sat down on the edge of a bunk. Ernie was running the meeting. Roy probably would have presided, because he had conducted the orientation Monday, but he had been called away. I noticed at once how quiet and attentive the boys were, at least in comparison to how they had been in meetings earlier in the week. Perhaps it was the effect of the candlelight, perhaps the result of a day of exercise in mountain air. Or perhaps something really had happened to them during the week. For whereas on Monday and Tuesday the teachers had to stop repeatedly and wait for the talking to stop, tonight the boys sat quietly and paid attention, and there were very few instances of the whispering, snickering, or scuffling that sixth-grade boys seem to bring with them into any group.

Ernie began by asking them what they had enjoyed most in camp. Many of the boys said they had liked the hikes best, especially the Indian village and the beaver valley (which I had not seen). Two of them mentioned geology, one pond biology, one wild life, and one fire sighting. One boy (it was hard to see who was talking, in the dim light) said he most enjoyed the stuff about sky and stars because he figured that some of them would be going up there one of these days. Someone else mentioned "food."

As my eyes adjusted to the candlelight I began to relate faces and names to voices. George and Yankees were sitting near Ernie. Almost exactly opposite Ernie was Dan, looking sullen but dominant as usual, seated as though to lead the opposition. I picked out John, hunching up his thin long body, Money-back and the Dice-maker and half a dozen others I knew.

And I picked out one small boy who had drawn my particular attention during the week. This was a lad I shall call Sandy. I had identified him, to my own satisfaction at least, as one of a small group from a special class of retarded children who had been brought to Cuyamaca this week. It is regular practice to bring both mentally and physically handicapped children to camp along with normal children. Six of these children, I believe, had been included. No one told us who they were; they were given a completely fresh start. Although I thought I could identify at least four of them, still I doubted that the other children did, and certainly there were few signs that they were set apart in any way. Little Sandy, for example, had been a Weatherbird and taken part in several of the activities I had joined. He had a little trouble with pronouncing some words plainly, but no one laughed at it, and in general the boys seemed to accept and even to take care of him. When he fell into the creek, on a class hike, they helped him out and brushed him off and did not make fun of him. When he got across the Monkey Bridge without falling off they patted him on the back. He seemed to be treated exactly as he was — a little less well coordinated, a little slower, but still a fellow whom you didn't object to having in your group and even liked to look after when necessary. I noticed particularly where Sandy was sitting in the meeting. On one side of him was the boy who had directed the song, and next to *him* the boy who had played the guitar. On the other side of Sandy was David, the boy who had been described to us as a "natural leader" but had got himself suspended from school, and had spent part of the first night at camp on the shower room bench. In other words, Sandy was seated in the midst of the group leadership.

Ernie asked what they would like to see changed about camp, and got a highly miscellaneous set of suggestions — more hikes, more play, let them stay in camp more than one week, and so on. He asked what they had learned in camp, and here the discussion moved along almost too smoothly. The comments seemed too pat and general: friendship, responsibility, conservation, the names of trees, and so on. But when Ernie asked, "What do you think you learned about yourself this week?" he seemed to push the right button.

The comments, unlike the previous ones, did not seem to be what the boys thought they were expected to say; rather they took on the tone of man-to-man talk, and quite the frankest I had heard all week.

"The toughest thing I had to learn" — it was the guitar player speaking — "was to go up to somebody I didn't know and say 'hello.' When I did it, it was all right, but I had a hard time doing it."

A boy spoke out of the shadows. I couldn't see his face. "I found I was kind of a slob in manners," he said. There was laughter around the circle, but it was not unkind laughter — rather the way that boys cover up a little embarrassment.

"I found I had to do my share of the work,'" said Yankees.

"Was that bad? Was there too much to do?" asked Ernie.

Most of them said no.

"Was it easier when you took turns and shared the work?" asked Ernie.

"Sure," they said. "Yes. Of course."

"Sometimes at home I hated work," said a big boy. "It was more fun here because everybody was doing it."

"I learned to keep quiet," said Money-back suddenly.

"Oh no, you didn't," said the guitar player.

"On activities?" asked Ernie.

"Yeah. Activitities. Meetings," said Money-back.

"I guess I learned to listen, too," said a voice I didn't recognize.

"I don't know, I guess though, I don't like to say it." It was Dice-maker speaking. He seemed to be having trouble getting the idea out, whatever it was. He finished it in a rush of words: "I guess I learned I was acting like a big mouth."

What was going on, I asked myself. Was this a kind of revival meeting? Did the boys feel they had to give "testimony"? But no, Ernie was not the evangelistic type. Most of what they were saying they must be sincere about, even though they might deny it the next week.

"I learned it wasn't so hard to stay with a lot of people," said little George.

"When I came to camp, I didn't much like being out in the open. No streetlights and stuff. But I do now. I think it's a good thing to get away from the city." This from another boy I didn't recognize.

"I think it's a good thing to get away from home for a few days," said another boy from the shadows.

"So you'll appreciate it more?" asked Ernie.

"I think I learned how to work with a group better than before," said the boy who had directed the song. "I guess I acted like a loner."

"It's the kind of thing you learn from football or basketball," said David.

"Teamwork," said another boy.

"I learned I could take showers without worrying about some-body watching," said a boy, with a little embarrassment. "Like you have something you don't want anybody to see."

There were a few snickers.

"I found I could take responsibility if I had to," said someone.

"What does responsibility mean to you?" asked Ernie.

There was a short silence.

"It's sort of like when someone depends on you because they know you can do it and you know you have to or you'll let them down."

"When there's no one to pick up after you, and you have to do it yourself."

"When you're a team, and everybody has to be part of it."

"That's very good," said Ernie. "When you sweep out more than your half of the cabin and do something like that for someone else, do you ever get a kind of good feeling about it?"

There wasn't much comment on this.

"What else did you learn about yourselves?" asked Ernie.

"When I first came, I daydreamed too much," said the boy beside Ernie. "I wasn't alert. But I got with it."

"Do you daydream too much in school, maybe?" said Ernie.

"Maybe," the boy admitted.

"Were there too many rules?" asked Ernie.

"You know —" The pause was a sign for everyone to look at the speaker. It was Dan. He himself was looking at the floor. Perhaps this was the loyal opposition I had waited for.

"You know, when I came on Monday," Dan said slowly, "I didn't want to do anything. Especially if anybody told me. Especially I didn't want to mind any rules. But now it's about over, I think maybe the rules were all right. Most of them. And I'd like to try again"

The full impact of that statement sank into me, and perhaps into the boys as well, because there was a silence.

"Let me ask you," said Ernie after a while. "If no teachers had been here would you have acted the same, or better, or worse?"

There was a flurry of answers, not all in agreement. The song leader said finally: "If there'd been a few of us, yes. With lots of us, I think we needed teachers around."

I left soon after that because I wanted to hear at least a sample of what the girls were saying in their meetings. But it was too late. The meeting in Westwind was just breaking up, and I judged from the last few minutes of it that it had followed pretty much the same direction as Northwind. The Eastwind meeting had already ended, and the girls were hearing a folk song record.

Back in the staff lounge, I asked some of the camp teachers and the classroom teachers what they made of the evaluation meetings.

"I wonder whether it made any difference to them to know they were being listened to?" said a teacher from San Diego.

I asked Harry whether an evaluation session was any different when they had visitors or when they didn't. He said the meetings vary so much that he doubted the visitors had too much effect on what was said. In general, he said, the meetings are pretty impressive performances and about in the same key we had heard tonight.

"I could hardly believe my ears," Dan's classroom teacher said. "I'll say this, though: Dan has acted different the last couple of days."

"Dave has been very decent, too," someone else added.

"A very likable boy," Harry said.

"He's a leader," the San Diego teacher said.

"I'll say this," said one of the La Mesa teachers. "I've been able to get closer to my pupils up here this week, and talk with them more frankly about their real feelings, than I was ever able to do at home. I'd say that what they were saying tonight was pretty honest. Maybe too honest. It came from real deep in them, and they might cover it up tomorrow. Maybe they'll regress when they get back home."

"You can say that again," said the San Diego teacher.

"I'd give anything," added the La Mesa teacher, "to be able to come up here with them early in the fall, and get started on this kind of relationship at the beginning of the school year."

I put the question that was bothering me to Dottie. "What do you think that performance added up to tonight?" I asked. "Was it a revival meeting and 'testimony,' or was it the real thing?"

"Probably some of both," she said. "But more the real thing. Something happens to them up here. It isn't just the facts they learn — after all, they aren't here for long. It's a point of view. It's a little bit of insight, perhaps. Maybe it doesn't last forever. But something happens. We see it every week."

I asked how the girls' meetings on Thursdays differed from the boys'.

"The boys are more physical, and the girls a little more vocal," Walt said.

"The girls have lots to say," said Harry.

"I think the boys are more honest," said Dottie. "The girls are more flowery — we had a wonderful week, and that type of thing. We're all such good friends now. That sort of thing."

"They cry together a little," chuckled Harry.

Later, while Walt and I were having a cup of coffee, I asked him what he saw happening to the boys and girls at camp.

"It gives them an opportunity to sort of stretch themselves," he said. "Some strange things happen to youngsters when they come to camp. Not just new, vital experiences in classwork, but new outlooks on the personality of their classmates, and new values for living with people."

With some fatherly pride, Walt said that he had a son coming to camp with the sixth grade next year, although he would probably go to one of the other camps rather than Cuyamaca. I suggested it would be interesting to see how one's own youngster reacts to the program. Was the boy looking forward to it, I asked.

"Oh, yes," said Walt. "He already wants to be a science teacher.

Then after working with the Forest Service this summer he wants to be a naturalist. He says, 'How can I do both?' But it will be interesting to see what he has to say when he has been to camp."

"What do most of them say?" I asked.

"Most of the time they write us about the fun they had. And that's all right. The Monkey Bridge is valuable for the simple reason that youngsters enjoy going across monkey bridges. Enjoyment should be a part of camp.

"Lots of the statements in a Thursday night session are usually about the opportunity to live together in a camp situation, have experiences together, and make new friends.

"When they get to recalling some of the other things they did, and things start falling into place, they'll talk about the conservation experience. This is one of the highlights of the camping program, and I suspect that the great value to San Diego County will be these youngsters growing up with that conservation experience."

I asked him about what effects he thought the classes had.

"What the youngsters speak about," he said, "is that they have a new experience, different from the classroom. Yet still and all, we're studying all the time, having assignments, working on projects in science, and it comes at them sort of subtly, you might say. It sneaks up on them, and they don't realize until the week is over that they have learned something and had a wonderful rich time."

"Do you see any personality changes during the week up here?" I asked him.

"Some of the youngsters come with adjustment problems," he said. "Some of our specials and maladjusted youngsters give us a real challenge. You have to take them from their experience and their background, and you try to discover something that can get close to them and then work from that. We're working with individuals that are always different. Sometimes it's not so rewarding as it would be in other situations, but sometimes it is too.

"I remember two years ago," he said, "we had a real problem youngster at camp. He gave us a great deal of trouble. He had been in four or five schools, and had a long record of trouble. His teacher was just at her wits' end. I fell heir to the job of helping him because he happened to be in my cabin. And I did get a chance to talk to him over the period of five days, and the head counselor talked to him, and other teachers did, and we began to see some results from it. We just happened to catch him when he was receptive. I got through to him. The next year his classroom teacher returned to camp and said the boy had just changed completely; he had become a different boy after the camp experience. They had two other boys they wanted me to take care of!

"You don't usually see that kind of change, but you do see changes. Some of the classroom teachers tell us they see things happen here they never thought was possible. It's the different setting, the different ground rules. They see a youngster come up and say 'thank you' to someone, and they've never heard him say that before."

I took my usual evening walk. The clouds had passed and the camp was bathed in magnificent moonlight. Every live oak branch on the mesa was almost as sharp as in daylight. In the east, near the moon, the sky was blue, almost aquamarine; from there toward the west it shaded into purple and black. The cabins were quiet. I walked and thought about the meeting. My guess was about like Dottie's. They had said things tonight they probably would never say out of this setting. They had been a little caught up in the spirit of confession and candlelight. Maybe they were saying, partly, what they thought was expected of them. But beyond that, they were taking off the lid from some thoughts that were usually hidden deeply. They were experiencing, at least some of them, a moment of insight, and because of the atmosphere they were willing to share it. They might not say the same things in class or even at home. But for a few moments there in the candlelight, in Northwind cabin, they were seeing some important things clearly.

## XII
## DAY OF DEPARTURE

FRIDAY WAS CONSTRUCTED ESPECIALLY to make visitors want to stay in the mountains forever. The air smelled as though it had been swept and dusted. The sky was deep blue; the clouds that floated over it, soft translucent white. The wind was light, dry, soft on the skin. The sun crept up over the mountain and fell like a friendly hand on our shoulders. Heavy jackets came off, and one or two boys turned cartwheels, out of sheer exuberance, in front of the flagpole.

When we gathered at the Hall of the Winds again, Marty introduced the children to "a little friend" — a pet kangaroo rat — and to her favorite trap that caught but did not kill animals. The children were full of questions, but for some reason most of the questions today came from the girls. I wondered whether the girls felt more like asking things of a female teacher, or whether it was a "girl topic." Anyway they asked: Where do you get traps like that? (Marty told them.) Won't the animals bite you when you let them out of the trap? (Use gloves.) What do you bait the traps with? (Chunky peanut butter, or peanut butter mixed with oatmeal.) Has that mouse — meaning the kangaroo rat — had babies? (No, it's *Mr.* Rat.) Why does my hamster smell like peanut butter? (Don't know, unless you feed him peanut butter.)

The Weatherbirds gave their last report of the week: Wind west at 4; temperature 60, low last night 40; humidity 40; barometer 29 inches and steady; fire danger medium high; forecast — the first confident one of the week — fair!

Everyone hummed the funeral march, and one of the La Mesa teachers — a curvy little woman with a bright smile — came forward to report on the cabin inspection. Northwind had slid back from their fine performance of Thursday. Apparently there had been a pillow fight, or something of that kind, Friday morning, and some beds were in disorder when the inspectors arrived. Their week's total was still a bit better than Southwind's, however, and, as one of the other visiting teachers said, none of us would have predicted that four days ago. Westwind was the winner for the week — half a point higher than Eastwind, five points higher than either of the boys. "That's what girls are good at," one of the boys said to me later. "Now if it had been tree sawing or bear shooting . . ."

Harry made his last talk to the assembly. He hoped they would

143

"Seconds, too."

take pleasant memories and a useful experience away with them. He hoped they would come back, to summer camp or to visit the Park. And some day, he said, I suppose your children will be coming here. (You can't say that to sixth graders without drawing a few snickers.) Lunch would be early today, Harry explained; the buses would leave shortly after noon. Friday morning would be an open choice for them. They could finish their crafts projects, or go on a tour of the State Park Indian museum, or take part in a "scavenger hunt," or a "woodquiz," or walk the Monkey Bridge, if they hadn't.

"Where are you going this morning?" George asked me.

"The Indian museum."

"I'll go with you," he said.

But first I wanted to visit Ill Wind, to see what kind of business nurse Carol had been doing. She had just finished caring for a cut and a cactus puncture. It had been an unusual week, she said, in that so many children had to be sent home: a total of six. The average was two or three. This was the height of an outbreak of communicable diseases in the schools, and four children had been sent home with suspicious symptoms of measles, mumps, or chicken pox. Two others had gone home with bad sore throats, one possibly strep. "We can't take any chances without a doctor in camp," said Carol. "If there's any real reason to suspect a communicable disease or something serious like appendicitis or a broken bone or a bad infection, we have to get the child out to a place where he can have proper care."

I asked her to tell me what happened in Ill Wind on a typical day.

"Let's take Wednesday," she said. "Start at 12:30 a.m. Don brought me one of his young fellows from Northwind who had thrown up in his sleeping bag. The poor kid upchucked twice more during the night. He had a sign of a rash, and a fever, and his mother came for him the next morning. He had been exposed to measles.

"Here's the record for the day," she said. "Look down the page and I'll fill in any details you need."

The log recorded that Carol had seen 18 patients that day in addition to the boy who got sick at night. The visits started before breakfast. A girl had come in, complaining of a stuffy nose. She had no temperature, so Carol had treated the symptoms — with mentholatum, gargle, and cough drops — and told the girl to come back if it didn't get better.

The period after breakfast was the chief sick call of the day. During this time, Carol saw:

A girl with a stomachache. She had no other symptoms, so Carol gave her a little soda mint.

A boy with a swollen ankle. He had twisted it yesterday. Carol wrapped it, gave him an ice pack, and told him to take it easy that day.

A boy with a splinter in the big toe of his right foot. Carol extracted it with tweezers, applied antiseptic and a band-aid, and checked to see that he'd had a tetanus shot recently.

A boy who reported back to let Carol see whether his bruised finger had become infected. It was getting along fine.

A girl with cold, headache, sore throat. No temperature. The nurse treated the symptoms, told her to come back.

A boy with symptoms of eczema. He had had it before, but thought it was getting worse now. Carol asked him what he did for it at home. He said he had a special medicine which he forgot to bring along. Carol advised him to wash clean and apply lanolin— and come back if it got worse.

A boy with a bloody nose. There had been a scuffle. Carol stopped the bleeding with ice, and reported the squabble to Harry.

That took care of the group who came just after breakfast. During the morning there were three other visitors:

A girl who had scraped her finger in the rock shop. Carol cleaned it, applied antiseptic and a band-aid, and warned the girl about keeping it clean.

A boy who had come to camp late. Carol took his temperature, explained the health rules to him, and recorded the admission.

Another boy with a splinter. Carol removed it.

Just after lunch a girl arrived with a hangnail which she feared was infected. Carol reassured her.

Another girl came in to have a dressing changed on a cut finger.

During the afternoon, a girl came in complaining about a stomach-ache (not entirely surprising considering the size of the meals I had seen consumed!). She had no other symptoms. She said she took Pepto Bismol for stomachaches at home, and Carol gave her a dose of it.

Another girl came with a scab knocked off and bleeding. Carol cleaned it and applied antiseptic and a band-aid.

A boy came in, apparently on the advice of a teacher, saying that he had had a headache earlier in the afternoon but felt all right now. No temperature. Carol told him to return if the headache came back.

After dinner, a boy came in with a badly scraped finger. Carol checked his record to make sure he had a recent tetanus shot, then dressed the finger.

A girl came in coughing and complaining of a cold. Carol took her temperature, treated the symptoms, and told her to check back if she felt worse.

"None of these happened to be very serious," said Carol. "My job is really to catch the serious ones and see that they get handled properly. In most of these cases today I was just trying to make sure that none of the little troubles blew up into big ones without us knowing about it. For instance, that the sore throat didn't develop into a bad one without the child telling us, or that one of the wounds didn't become infected. That's why I told so many of them to come back if they felt worse, or to come back to have something checked."

We were interrupted by a buxom girl who announced that she had a stomachache. Carol popped the thermometer into her mouth and I went to join the museum trip.

Augie and Jay were the teachers in charge of the museum group. Augie wasted no time starting to talk about Indians.

"Have you ever thought about where they came from?" he asked. "They were here when the Europeans came. Were they always here, —or did they come from somewhere else before the European settlers came?"

"They came from someplace," said a red-haired girl, rather doubtfully.

"Do you all agree with that?"

They nodded.

"That's very interesting," said Augie. "Let's sit down a minute and talk about it. I wonder how people ever found that out. Do you have any idea, Jimmie?"

"I don't know," said Jimmie.

"They wouldn't leave tracks, would they?" said Augie.

"No," they laughed.

"How do we know that Christopher Columbus and the Puritans and the Spanish priests like Father Junipero Serra came here?" Augie asked.

"They wrote about it," said George.

"Other people wrote about it too," said a little girl.

"Did the Indians have any written history?" asked Augie.

"No."

"That's right," said Augie. "And at the time we're talking about — many thousands of years ago — they must have had no written language. Now think about it a minute. Suppose you're a scientist and you're trying to solve this problem. You haven't any history to depend on. What kind of evidence could you look for?"

They furrowed their brows.

"Well, let's take an example," said Augie. "Suppose you saw a foreign-looking man coming out of the airport. How could you get some information on where he came from without asking him? How could you make a good guess as to whether he was, let's say, a Japanese or a Chinese or an Italian or an African or something else?"

"You could find out if he speaks Italian," suggested a girl with a blue ski-coat.

"Right," said Augie. "What else?"

"Maybe he looks like a Japanese or Italian or something."

"Good. Now even if this stranger had been born in this country of a Japanese father, he might still look a bit Japanese, wouldn't he?" asked Augie.

"Yes."

"Or even if his family had been in this country several generations, he might still look a little bit Japanese?"

"Oh, yes."

"But wait a minute," said Augie. "These Indians must have come to this continent thousands of years ago. Would they still have any signs of the family of people they came from?"

They were fascinated by this problem. If this had happened Monday, they might not have risen to the bait. Over the intervening days, however, they had learned to like these little problems. They asked Augie whether scientists didn't have any ways to tell about where the Indians might have come from, and he explained that they could measure heads and bodies and such things, and they had found that the American Indians had some resemblance to Asian people. How about the language? That evidence wasn't so clear. What other kinds of evidence could be used to find out whether they might or might not have come from Asia? "Well," drawled Augie, "let's go back to this foreign looking gentleman. Could you tell anything about his origin by how he acted? Or what he brought with him? Or what stories or songs he knew?" They understood: Maybe some of the customs of the American Indians, or some of the tools they used, or some of their stories might resemble some of the peoples of Asia. But how could they have come from Asia? "Walked?" suggested the boy named Jimmie. "Over the Pacific?" asked Augie. They worked out the idea that the Indians might have come over the ice between Siberia and Alaska.

"One more hike before going home."

"But wait a minute! wait a minute!" said Augie. He liked to jerk them up that way. "How do we know that they didn't go the other way — that people weren't here first and went to Asia?"

The red-haired girl had an answer for that after a while. "Can't we find out whether there are older things over there than here?" And Augie said that was good thinking, and the evidence was all in favor of human civilization being older in Asia than in the Americas.

It was a fascinating exercise to watch, and the children seemed to enjoy it. Anyway, Augie said that the best evidence scientists could get indicated that the Indians did come from Asia, probably over the ice, and scattered to every part of North and South America. Why were there *different* kinds of Indians, then? One of the reasons was that the Indians adapted to their environment. If they were in different environments they had to live differently to get along well in those environments. Let's take a trip, he said. An imaginary trip. Imagine that it's a thousand years ago, and we are traveling over North America. Start with New England, he said. He took them over to creekside.

"Imagine the creek is the ocean," he said. "You're in New England. Has anybody ever been to the East Coast? Anybody have an idea what kind of climate it has?"

"Awful," said a good Californian.

Hot in summer, cold in winter, they said.

"What kind of clothes do you think the Indian would wear, then?"

He wouldn't wear much in summer, but in winter he would need fur clothing.

"And what kind of home would he need?" After they talked about that for a minute, Augie got out a picture of an Iroquois long house, and showed it. "They were farmers," he said. "They didn't travel around. They built forts and warm houses.

"Now," he said, "let's travel west across the Alleghenies and the Mississippi." He took them over a little hillock and came down again beside the creek, which he said was the western side of the Mississippi.

Here, they decided, the climate would be different from New England. The plains were dry and hot in the summer, and flat.

"What were some of the tribes out here?"

They named the Sioux, but Augie had to tell them of the Cheyenne and Arapahoe.

"If you lived on the plains, what animals would help determine your life?"

"You could dress in hides," suggested a girl.

"You could ride horses."

"When the horse was introduced, he helped change the Indians' lives. How would a horse change life for you if you had lived there?"

They said the Indian would have transportation to travel long distances.

"Suppose you were a buffalo," said Augie. "How would a horse change *your* life?"

"Why, then the Indian could follow me around," said the red-haired girl, blushing a little.

"Would the plains Indian live in one place, then, or would he travel around?" And, after they answered that:

"Would he live in a house or something he could carry with

him?"

"Now we'll go to the Southwest," he said, and led them on, another hundred yards — always moving in the general direction of the museum. He got them to describe the Southwest — desert country, mostly flat, water the most important possession. They named three tribes — Apache, Comanche, and Navajo — and Augie added the Hopi to the list.

"What could the Southwest Indians make their houses of?" asked Augie.

"Rocks," said a straw-haired girl.

"Adobe," said the girl with the ski-coat.

"High or low houses?"

"Open," said a boy.

"High." This was the girl with the green coat. "Like apartment houses."

"Why?"

"Because of their enemies. They climbed up with ladders and kept their enemies out."

"And adobe was cool."

"What did the Southwest Indians make that people still like to go down there to buy?"

They knew about blankets and pottery.

"Why were pottery bowls so important to those Indians?"

The children guessed that they were needed to save water.

The next stop, a hundred yards farther on, was the Northwest and the creek had now become the Columbia basin. They talked about the climate, and the clothes that would be needed, and what the Indians would have to eat. Augie emphasized the importance of animals in Indian history — the fish, whales, dogs, oxen, caribou, and so forth. Then he led them to the end of their cross-continental trek, in front of the museum, which he said was California.

"Why did so many Indians live in California?"

"The weather?"

Augie smiled. We went into the museum. It was unattended, but Augie had a key. The building itself was a stucco house, the lower floor of which had been refinished with good lights and glass museum cases. The exhibits were really quite good. They included the food, clothing, and shelter of the local Indian tribes, some of their recreational equipment, their art, household articles, a good relief map of the area, and a reconstruction of the old Stonewall Gold Mine. The children were fascinated by the food exhibit. Jay told them that pieces of poison oak were said to have been put in the middle of the acorn meal to gain immunity to it; and that the pieces of stone accidentally ground up in the meal were responsible for wearing off the teeth of the Indians.

"Here's an arrow point like the one I found," said a boy.

"And you can see here what they made most of their arrows out of," said Jay. "See — obsidian, quartz, and chert."

There was a case of pipes. "What did they smoke in their pipes?" asked Augie.

"Pot?" asked a boy.

"LSD," said another, getting into the spirit of things. Augie laughed and let it go.

"Come outside now," he said a little later, "and look around you. What trees or plants do you see that you could use if you were Indians?"

I hadn't been very enthusiastic about going to the museum. It couldn't have been anything but anticlimax after the preceding days. But I was glad I had gone, because, although it wasn't the best activity of the week, it summed up for me what I had come to think of as the camp school style. For one thing, although the camp was in this wonderful recreational country, it wasn't recreation that went on there; it was education. It really was school transported to the mountains. The teaching had a quality of its own, too. It was built on priming the students with questions, getting them to be alert, and then challenging them to find answers themselves. And at the end of the museum visit I saw two other things that were indisputably a part of the camp style. Three boys were given large brooms to sweep out the museum. "Let's keep it clean for the next visitors," said Augie. And he took care of a discipline problem with the combination of firmness and kindness which I had seen before in the teachers. He had punished a boy for being noisy and rude, by making him sit outside the museum while the rest of the party went through. Afterward, he excused himself, and while Jay shepherded the rest of us back toward camp he counseled with the boy and gave him a five-minute personal tour through the museum.

I detoured by way of the Monkey Bridge. The children were walking across on the middle rope, holding tight to the higher ropes with either hand. I heard the chorus of squeals, laughter, catcalls, and shouts when I was still 200 feet away. The boys and girls made their way across, with teachers watching carefully and their fellow campers watching mirthfully. Some practically ran across; for others it was a long and tortuous trip. I saw a girl lose her nerve in the middle, and hold on desperately while she was encouraged to complete the crossing. No one made fun of her.

Back in camp, the scavengers were dashing around looking for a needle from a Jeffrey pine, a piece of igneous rock, and so forth. Pieces of manzanita were shining in the sun as the crafts workers put final loving touches on them. The bedrolls and suitcases were packed and in front of the dormitories.

But the big news of the day, the tidings that drew a chuckle from everyone, and passed through the camp grapevine almost with the speed of light, came to us just before lunch: Jennie had fallen into the creek!

She had been with a group of children on the bank of the creek, not far from Rock Canyon, and — in some ill-guided moment she wouldn't soon forget — had taken one step too close. The details were passed along with chuckles and knee-slaps. "Off the Monkey Bridge?" someone would ask. "No, in Rock Canyon?" "Rock Canyon?" Lithe, agile Jennie, of all people, had slid down a slippery rock into a three-foot pool of water, from which she emerged, dripping mud, frigid mountain water, and embarrassment.

"What did the boys and girls do?"

"Helped her up the bank."

"Nobody said 'good dive'?"

"Oh, no!"

Not because of any lack of affection for Jennie, it was made clear, was the story circulated with such joyous speed. On the contrary, the incident forged a bond of fellow-feeling between every camper and Jennie. But she seemed to feel the result was hardly worth it.

Lunch was a rather subdued meal, despite the news from Rock Canyon. Most children that age aren't good at final speeches or goodbyes, and I think most of them were genuinely sad to leave camp.

"What do you think you'll remember longest from camp?" I asked at the lunch table.

"Food," said long John.

"The banana pudding?" a girl asked him.

"I liked the chop suey," said Maria.

"I didn't," said Sally.

"You'll remember something besides the food, won't you?" I asked.

"The Monkey Bridge," said Money-back.

"It sure swings sometimes," said a little girl.

"I'll remember singing," said Maria.

"I think I'll remember just getting out into things," said a boy. "It isn't like reading about it. You can touch it, and see it. Kind of live with it."

"Crafts were fun," said Sally.

"The Indian village."

"The beaver canyon."

"I liked it when we sat still and listened out there to the sound of the forest," a blue-eyed girl said. "We sat real still and listened to things I'd never heard before. I don't think I had. Even the wind coming up — I could hear that."

"The deer that jumped out."

"I'll remember the whole camp," said one of the boys, "except washing dishes and sweeping up the cabin."

"Didn't you like the work?" I asked him.

"*I* liked it," said Maria.

"He's wrong," said Yankees, who had been rather quiet. "It was fun. And it was good for us. And it's easy to make friends when you're doing dishes."

"Jennie had us sing when we were cleaning up the cabin," said Maria.

"I wish they'd let the kids go around more by themselves," said Sally.

"Yeah, they didn't have to be *that* strict," said John.

This started a little discussion. "They weren't too strict." "They were real nice." "Well, maybe, but they had to, to keep things running." And so forth. But if I had been a camp teacher, listening to the talk, I would have felt pretty good. Especially, I think, when John, lanky, withdrawn John, said something I don't believe he would have been capable of saying on Monday:

"I thought some of them were real right guys," he said. "I felt real warm and close toward some of them. Roy and Ernie, for instance. I felt real good towards them."

I asked them whether they had missed television at camp. If they had, they wouldn't admit it.

We sat and talked a little more, and went outside with the suitcases. I remembered what Harry had told me at the beginning of the week: a day of orientation; three big days of science, crafts, hikes, and conservation; and a day getting ready to leave. This was a downhill day, all right. The youngsters felt it, and there wasn't much horseplay while they waited for the buses to come.

They came around the curve, their stainless steel trim shining in the sun. The bedrolls and suitcases were loaded, the children were loaded, goodbyes were said. The last thing I saw as they pulled out was little George's face at the window, his mouth saying what I thought was "Goodbye, Doc!" The last thing I heard, as the bus disappeared in the pines, was the beginning of a camp song, sung lustily by a combination of uncertain sopranos and almost baritones —

— I like the forest, I like the chaparral . . .

I said my own goodbyes, and drove out of camp around the big curve onto route 79. I looked back along the row of peaks, where the same scenario was probably being enacted in two other camps I knew. Buses were probably coasting around the switchbacks on the west face of Mount Palomar, down from the wooded heights around Camp Marston to the plateau land beyond Julian. Like the Cuyamaca buses, they were heading purposefully toward the coastal plains, carrying full loads of children who felt a little sad and let down now that the adventure was over, but more confident and more experienced and browner than they had been a week ago. They would be singing for a while, and then remembering. At each of the camps, at that moment, brief meetings would be convening. The teachers at Marston would be asking jokingly, "Did we win, Tom?", and at all three camps the head counselors would be asking, "What did we learn this week to keep in mind later?" Soon a second wave of migration would take off toward the coast—Ernie's red Porsche, and the pickup truck, and two Volkswagens, Fords and Chevvies and motorcycles — carrying the camp staffs to their weekends. In a few hours the camps would be repopulated with week-end campers, who would put *their* sleeping bags and bedrolls on the bunks, climb the mesas, sing around the campfire, and perhaps — some of them — half freeze one of *their* feet in the unfamiliar cold of a mountain night. And then, Monday morning, it would all start over again. Back into camp with the Porsche, the pickup, the motorcycles, and the others. Back to the morning teachers meeting. Back to preparing the kitchen for 160 hungry children. And then, at 9:45 or so, a row of camp teachers waving to the incoming buses.

I wondered if I wouldn't miss it a bit, next week. But I drove on out of the mountain scenery, down the slopes toward the freeway, back to the coastal plains and the city.

# XIII
# A LOOK BEHIND THE SCENES

LATER I RETURNED to San Diego to find out what kind of organization and effort lay behind the camps.

While my airplane was swooping down, past Oceanside and La Jolla, I wrote myself a few notes that read like this:

*How is it organized?*
*What does it cost, and who pays?*
*How do they coordinate all of it?*
*How does the community react to it?*

On the third floor of the big County Administration Center, where the Camp Commission has its offices and where the windows open on harbor sounds and sea air, Edwin Pumala and Denver Fox smiled a little over my notes, and said they could answer the first two questions for me. As for the last one, they said, they would advise me to talk to some community leaders — the Superintendent of Schools, for example, whose district puts a large chunk of tax money into the program, members of the City Council and the County Board of Supervisors, and perhaps the county PTA President. The question about coordination, they said, was truly an important one for such a complex program; perhaps the best way to get a sense of how it worked would be to attend a meeting of the Camp Commission itself, and the Education Advisory Committee.

As they explained the organization to me, it seemed simple in terms of the complex job it is asked to do.

To put it briefly, there is an overall coordinating body called the San Diego City-County Camp Commission. This has been created by ordinance, and its five members represent the San Diego City Council, the San Diego County Board of Supervisors, the Superintendent of the San Diego City Schools, the San Diego County Superintendent of Schools, and the Ninth District Parent Teachers County Council which in turn represents Parent Teachers Associations and parents throughout San Diego County. Edwin Pumala, as Director of Camping and Executive Director of the Camp Commission, is the executive officer of this group.

There is also an Outdoor Education Advisory Committee, representing the participating school districts, George Hall, Associate Superintendent of San Diego Schools, is chairman of this group, and Denver Fox, as Principal of the Camp Schools, is the executive officer.

The division of responsibility between these two working groups is based on the fact that the schools are responsible for instruction in the school camps. This responsibility is delegated to the Outdoor Education Advisory Committee, and the Camp Principal. Ultimately, he is responsible for nomination of certificated teaching staff, determination of curriculum, providing of teaching materials, and day-to-day operation of a school that each year enrolls more than 15,000 students.

The Camp Commission is responsible for coordinating all the uses of the camps, and all the avenues of community support that make the camps and their programs possible. In addition to the 15,000 to 17,000 sixth-grade children who come to camp each year as a part of the outdoor education program, another 8,000 adults and children come to week-end or summer camping programs. The Camp Commission is directly responsible for the arrangements for and staffing of these week-end and summer camps. It is responsible for buildings and capital equipment at the camps, for new construction like that at Cuyamaca and Palomar, for leasing camps when that is necessary as it is at Marston, for providing the supporting services at the camps — food, health, maintenance, clerical — and in general for keeping the accounts and handling the funds that come in from city, county, parents of children who go to school camps, and all other camp users.

Membership of the Camp Commission and the Outdoor Education Advisory Committee interlock. Dr. Hall, who serves as chairman of the Education Advisory Committee, also represents the Superintendent of San Diego City Schools on the Camp Commission; and Pumala and Fox participate in the meetings of both groups.

I have drawn a few charts in the hope that they might make some of these relationships clearer. They may bear little resemblance to any official table of organization, but I hope they will give some idea of how the mechanism works in practice.

The characteristic of the organization which these charts do not catch is the community-wide nature of participation. For example, many civic and voluntary organizations make contributions — "camperships" to enable children to go to camp even though their parents cannot afford the cost; contributions to improve facilities; and the like. Many organized groups go to camps on weekends or in the summer. All the cooperating school systems participate in decisions regarding the instructional program. And parents throughout the county contribute to the cost of their childrens' food and transportation, for the school camps. In this kind of structure, therefore, "coordination" is much more than protocol

# ORGANIZATION OF THE CAMP COMMISSION

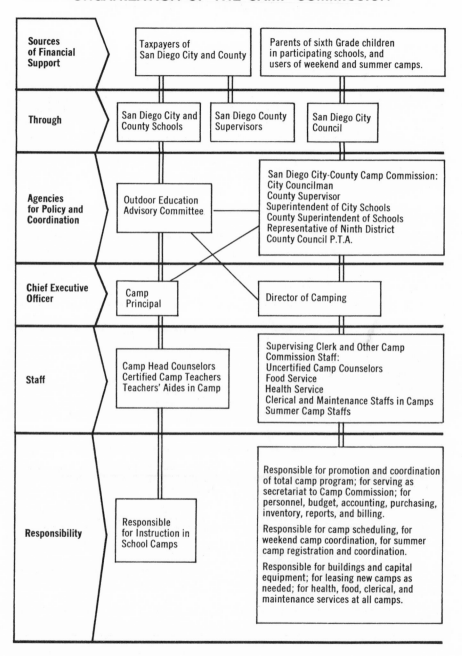

| Sources of Financial Support | Taxpayers of San Diego City and County | Parents of sixth Grade children in participating schools, and users of weekend and summer camps. |

Through — San Diego City and County Schools | San Diego County Supervisors | San Diego City Council

Agencies for Policy and Coordination — Outdoor Education Advisory Committee | San Diego City-County Camp Commission: City Councilman / County Supervisor / Superintendent of City Schools / County Superintendent of Schools / Representative of Ninth District County Council P.T.A.

Chief Executive Officer — Camp Principal | Director of Camping

Staff — Camp Head Counselors / Certified Camp Teachers / Teachers' Aides in Camp | Supervising Clerk and Other Camp Commission Staff: / Uncertified Camp Counselors / Food Service / Health Service / Clerical and Maintenance Staffs in Camps / Summer Camp Staffs

Responsibility — Responsible for Instruction in School Camps | Responsible for promotion and coordination of total camp program; for serving as secretariat to Camp Commission; for personnel, budget, accounting, purchasing, inventory, reports, and billing.

Responsible for camp scheduling, for weekend camp coordination, for summer camp registration and coordination.

Responsible for buildings and capital equipment; for leasing new camps as needed; for health, food, clerical, and maintenance services at all camps.

‖ Channels of financial support

157

# ORGANIZATION OF THE
# OUTDOOR EDUCATION PROGRAM

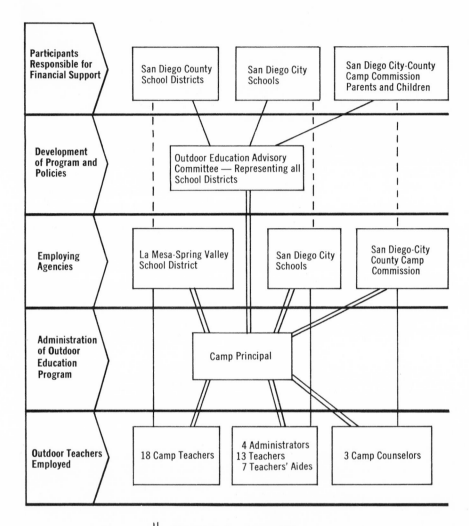

Lines of authority and responsibility

# FINANCIAL SUPPORT FOR THE CAMP PROGRAMS

| Kind of Cost | Cost of School Camp Operation | Cost of School Camp Instruction | Cost of Buildings and Capital Equipment | Cost of Weekend and Summer Camp Operation |
|---|---|---|---|---|
| **Source of Funds** | Parents and Children | 14 Participating School Districts | San Diego City and San Diego County | Campers or Sponsoring Organizations |
| **Agency Administering Funds** | San Diego City-County Camp Commission | Shared by La Mesa-Spring Valley and San Diego Unified School Districts | San Diego City-County Camp Commission | San Diego City-County Camp Commission |
| **Kinds of Services Paid for** | Accident Insurance Clerical Food Health Transportation Utilities | Teachers' Salaries Instructional Materials and Supplies Production | Housing Leasing of Camps | Clerical Counselors Food Health Transportation Utilities |

and politeness. It has to work!

"That's the way it's organized," they said to me. "Now what? Economics?"

They helped me draw another chart, which I have put in the book. This is what it says:

San Diego City and County share the capital costs, and the administrative costs of the Camp Commission itself.

The participating school districts share the cost of instruction.

The users of the camps — the parent of the children in the school camps; the week-end and summer campers, or their sponsoring organizations — pay the cost of camp operation except for instruction. In cases where parents are unable to pay some or all of the cost of sending their children to school camp, it is often possible to make up the needed money by gifts from civic organizations or individuals.

The parents of a sixth-grade child who goes to camp are asked to pay $15 for food and lodging, $3.25 for bus transportation to and from camp, and 35 cents for accident insurance — a total of $18.60.

The cost to participating school districts is presently $22.00 per child. This pays for teacher salaries and instructional equipment.

Adding in the contribution of the City and County, the total cost in tax money to operate the school camps is a little under $25 per child. Together with the parents' contribution, the cost is between $40 and $45 per child. This does not include a figure for amortizing original capital costs. Any school, city, or county going into such a program would have to take into account the cost of buildings and land.

The total budget of the camping programs — counting what comes from tax money, what is paid by parents and campers, and what comes as gifts — is edging up toward a million dollars a year. Somewhat less than half of this is tax money. The cost of sending 15,000 children to school camp is nearly $675,000, of which a little over $350,000 is tax money.

When I had a chance, I asked Dr. Ralph Dailard, Superintendent of San Diego Schools, how hard he had to defend adding costs of such magnitude to the school budget. (Instructional costs are shared by participating schools in proportion to sixth-grade enrollments, and San Diego City has more than half the enrollment.) He pointed out that the school program in California averages about $600 per child, and that $22 extra per sixth-grade child would increase the overall average by less than two dollars. A school district has to take on new programs as they are needed, he said; for example, San Diego is now putting $400,000 a year into educational television. And either sum, he noted with a smile, is peanuts beside the $30 million the city has just put into a new stadium.

Leaning back in his chair, he spoke softly and thoughtfully about the disappearing opportunities for children to have direct experience with nature, and about the growing ideas of time and progress flexibility in schools. "Some day," he said, "we may think of schooling as occurring anywhere, not just in school buildings. We talk now about San-San, a city from Santa Barbara to San Diego, or San Francisco to San Diego. And about a Chicago-Great Lakes complex, and a Washington-New York-Boston complex. If we don't have means of getting youngsters out of those great metropolitan jungles, they will grow up not knowing anything about nature or the world outside cities. We have found youngsters living here in the Southeast section who have never seen the Pacific ocean. They've seen the harbor, but they've never seen a tide pool; they've never heard the surf break. We'll be trapping people in these asphalt jungles of the future, unless we find a way to get them out to have meaningful experiences in another kind of environment, and the school is the only agency I see through which this can be accomplished."

The problem, therefore, he said, is not so much the cost as the quality of the program. "Did you know," he asked, "that we started with the assumption that if we sent a class and its teacher up there, then with minimal extra support we could have a school camping program? But the ordinary sixth-grade teacher was not prepared to deal with 20 or 30 students on a 24-hour basis and do any teaching of nature. We found we had to have a staff of camp teachers.

The instructional program has improved through the years, he said, and has become vital and more meaningful to the children. "This is real experience," he said. "Everyone who makes a new effort in education comes back to the realization that real learning is tied to real and vital experiences. So on philosophical grounds this is the soundest form of education. Not only does it add the dimension of getting out into nature and practicing conservation by digging bugs out of trees: It's in every respect just good education!"

I inquired whether there had been times when San Diego had considered eliminating the outdoor education program.

"Twice in the last 15 years," he said, "we faced the problem coming up of a tax ceiling where the finances were limited and we could only raise so much money until the tax level was voted. Each time we could see that some cutback was necessary, and it was necessary to face that squarely. Among other things that were list-ed for review has been the camping program. But it has not been cut. There has been no inclination to cut it, and strong resistance from the public against cutting it. One of the amazing things about the camping program has been almost overwhelming public and parental support of the program. We've had some who objected to it, some Council members, some members of the Board of Supervisors, who came on the Camp Commission determined that their role in life was to get rid of that particular piece of budget. And after a time they became solid supporters of the program."

"Would it be politically unwise to be against the camping program?" I asked.

"*I* think it is politically unwise," he said, "and these people are *convinced.* They get out to camps and see what happens to the youngsters and talk to the parents and become strong supporters. I could hardly name two groups that exist here that enjoy the amount of unequivocal support the camping program has."

I asked whether there had been any particular problems in bringing about the cooperation of so many civic and governmental organizations in the program.

"Through the years," he said, "there has been the problem of defining the roles of each of the agencies that were involved, and the use of their funding. Obviously the capital plant has to come from the city and county. The certificated staff has to come from the school districts. There was an issue for some years as to who

"How can you arrange the twigs for a one-match fire?"

would provide the nurses, cooks, maintenance men, and so forth. There were hard times for a while deciding where the responsibility for each of these should lie, before it was straightened out in practice and there was agreement that there should be four contributors — the city, the county, the school districts, and the parents — and the responsibilities should be carried out in the most efficient ways. At one time the County maintenance men went to the mountains on call if we needed an electrician, for instance, and this was a pretty expensive business until it was agreed that a certain number of maintenance men would be assigned. Another problem was the line of responsibility between the camping director, Mr. Pumala's office, and the school principal. As you know, we in the schools are under compulsion of law that the students must always be under the direction of a certificated employee. But all these have been worked out by men of good will."

He suggested, as had Fox and Pumala, that I attend a meeting of the Camp Commission and of the Education Advisory Committee to see how the charts got translated into people and actions. We checked the schedule of meetings. The Advisory Committee met a week befor the Commission. So the next Tuesday I turned up at the Outdoor Education Advisory Committee.

They met in a room not far from the Superintendent's office, in the Administration Building, around a long shiny blonde table, put together from smaller shiny blonde tables. The partitions that separated the meeting room from the hall and the adjoining rooms were light colored wood, the bearing walls were painted light green, and the windows had cream-color Venetian blinds. At one end of the room was a sink with built-in cabinets and a box of paper towels. Not inappropriately, the room had a school-like look.

Fourteen people were present, in addition to a secretary and me. Dr. Hall was presiding. He is a tall, balding man, with a big voice, and a friendly, no-nonsense manner that keeps a meeting going forward and, as a matter of fact, carried that particular meeting through 14 agenda items in an hour.

He introduced the members of the committee for my benefit. They were mostly principals of elementary schools or superintendents of districts in the county. As I recall, four of them came from schools in San Diego, and four or five from school systems outside San Diego city. There were two members of the administrative staff of the county superintendent of schools, and a regional elementary education director. There was Denver Fox, as principal of the camp schools, and Ed Pumala, as director of camping. Five of these people, Hall said — a man from Oceanside, on the northern edge of the county; a man from Chula Vista, at the southern edge of the county near the Mexican border; Fox, Pumala, and himself — had been members of the committee since it was first established by ordinance.

He introduced a new member of the committee: a representative of the larger of two districts that were just entering the program. The 1500 additional campers who would come from these districts would make it necessary to lease a fourth camp, at least temporarily. The problem of activating the outdoor education program at this new camp was one of the chief concerns of the present meeting. The other chief concern was the new construction at Camp Cuyamaca and Camp Palomar, and what it meant for the educational program.

The chairman called on Pumala to report on the status of the building project. Pumala said it was on schedule. The joint powers agreement that would permit the sale of $1,500,000 worth of bonds was being written. The architect's general plans had been approved by the State (because the construction was in State parks), by the City, and by the County.

"What are the tentative occupancy dates?" asked Hall.

Pumala said that the architect estimated the job could be done in six months. This was an iffy estimate. It could be done in six months if a large construction company was the successful bidder, and if the ongoing program did not interfere much with the construction work.

You could see concern building up in the educators around the table; they knew that heavy construction work did not mix well with outdoor school activities. The chairman asked Fox to talk about the problem of operating camp schools while the construction was going on.

He, too, was concerned, although he said that it was hoped most of the heavy work could be done in the summer when the camp schools were not in session. The most severe problem, he thought, would be providing a dining hall during the time when these buildings were being enlarged and remodeled. Someone suggested wryly that the camps might go on C-rations. Fox chuckled a little about that, and said it was a new idea. Field kitchens had been suggested, but not C-rations. Anyway, he thought the problem could be handled by temporarily moving the kitchen equipment, and the dining tables and chairs, to other buildings.

One committee member asked whether it would be necessary to retain a fourth camp after the new buildings at Cuyamaca and Palomar were in use. Fox said that the new construction would allow each of these camps to house 200 children, and he estimated that this would take care of the district's projected needs for about two years. This led to questions about whether 200 is too many for a good camp school program.

Obviously, the matter had already received a good deal of thought. "From the program point of view," Fox said, "the optimum would be to go ahead and run small camps. But that involves the problem of unit costs, and the degree of efficiency in use of facilities. These are important to the Camp Commission. It would also be desirable to have many small cabins, so as to have intimate relationships and high morale. But this would wear out the staff in night supervision, which is their main bugaboo and probably the main reason why teachers leave the camps. Furthermore, the smaller the groups, the more that children may have to pay to come to camp."

Decisions on size necessarily have to be compromises among these different values, he said.

"But at what point does it become dangerously poor education?" asked Hall.

They talked about what could be done to retain as many as possible of the advantages of small groups in relatively large camps. Each dormitory in the new camp construction would house 56 children, but in four separate rooms of 14 each. Fox explained one teacher could supervise all four of these. Activities could and would be kept small. "The only place where we may feel the increased size is in general meetings and at meals," he said.

This is the way the meeting went. There was a careful division between the responsibility of the Camp Commission and of this Outdoor Education Advisory Committee. In a sense, the Commission's concern was the school *camps;* the Committee was concerned with camp *schools.* When there was a question of facilities, or capital costs, or the overall program, Edwin Pumala was always called on; when the question dealt with the educational program or the teaching staff, Denver Fox or another representative from the schools talked about that.

So it was with the problem of leasing the fourth camp. The additional 1500 students from the two new districts had not been expected or budgeted for, and the only way to provide a school camp experience for them this year would be to lease additional facilities. They had settled on Camp Davidson, which was used on weekends and throughout the summer by the Girl Scouts but would be available for a school camp during the weekdays in the school year. The chairman asked Pumala about the progress of leasing arrangements.

The lease had been easy to arrange for, Pumala said. It would cost the City of San Diego and the County Board of Supervisors each $2,000, for 15 weeks. He said frankly that there was some concern on the Camp Commission as to how the City Council would react to paying for leasing Camp Davidson in order to help two school districts outside the city limits. "I am informed, though," he said, "that the Council will take up the matter this morning, and no trouble is expected."

Then came the educational questions from around the table: How about the staff? How large would it have to be? Could the experienced teachers be shared so that the children would not have both a new camp and a new staff? How about the facilities for the teaching program and staff living?

Most of these questions were directed to Denver Fox. Two experienced teachers would be assigned to the new camp from each of the three existing camps, and a camp teacher who has had considerable experience as a substitute head counselor would be the new head counselor. Thus in the new camp there will be some teachers new to outdoor education, but a core of experience in the staff. The capacity of the camp would be 93 children, and the usual ratio of one teacher to 10 children would be maintained. (He reminded them that this ratio was based on a 24-hour, rather than a school day, assignment.) Thus there would be nine teachers, a head counselor, a nurse, and food and maintenance staffs. They would get along without a camp clerk, to save money.

Facilities would be entirely satisfactory for the educational program, but the staff housing would leave something to be desired. Because the proprietors of Camp Davidson wanted to retain some of the housing, the staff would have to live out of suitcases and take their clothes and supplies away on weekends. The staff quarters would be less desirable than in the other camps, he said, and he hoped that they still had lots of pioneers working for them.

The new member from El Cajon Valley District reported on what his district was doing to get ready to use Camp Davidson. Parents were being informed about the outdoor education program; many of them were seeing a slide program. The first four weeks of the program had been scheduled. Teachers were preparing their pupils for the experience. He said there was a shortage of teaching kits, which the Advisory Committee provides, and several people around the table promised to lend some to the new districts.

They turned to the discussion of camperships. These are financial assistance to children whose parents cannot afford the whole cost of sending them to school camp. Pumala reviewed some of the history of this program for the benefit of the new members. "Over the years," he said, "the schools and the Camp Commission have held to the objective that every youngster should have an opportunity to go to his school camp, even though he does not have the money and his parents cannot find any way to provide it. So a campership program by the participating schools has been a part of the program since its inception. It was first on a local level, a school level. Then it was made a district problem. Now it has evolved so that the communities have asked not only the state but also the federal government for funds for this purpose. It is a sizable amount of money. When the Office of Economic Opportunity funds were available, it approached a hundred thousand dollars.

"Unfortunately," he said, "the OEO notified San Diego that there woud be no funds available this year. Then each one of the campership committees had to work out the best solution they could."

"As we had been doing it prior to two years ago when the federal financing came into being," noted Hall.

Members of the Committee began to talk about what they had done, and what else could be done, to fill the need. Apparently, things had been going pretty well, but considerably less easily than when OEO funds had been available. A man from the San Diego City schools reported that their campership fund at the beginning of the year was $3400, mostly contributed by the PTA, some women's clubs, the community service agency, certain industries, and a few individuals. This fund is available to schools on evidence of need. In addition, he said, Downtown Rotary was providing camperships for 20 pupils.

The principal of a school in a disadvantaged neighborhood said that about 20 to 30 of his 116 sixth graders would be unable to go to camp without financial help. The PTA maintains a campership fund of $100, but the school would have to go to the district for help, and even that might not be enough. Someone commented that unfortunately in the communities where the schools have the greatest need, the PTAs are least affluent.

Someone else reported that one school held a paper drive and used the proceeds to help a less affluent school with its campership needs.

The impression that came from this part of the meeting was of schools and some community organizations working very hard to make it possible for all their sixth graders to go to camp.

They disposed of some smaller matters, and then came to the matter of next year's finances. For the sake of committee members who had not previously seen the process, Hall explained how the charge per student is arrived at each year. He said that a subcommittee of the Outdoor Education Advisory Committee meets in

"Out where the wind smells swept and dusted."

April or May, together with the accountant from the City school system, the assistant superintendent for business from the County school office, and the accountant from the La Mesa-Spring Valley school district, which is the hiring agent for the participating school districts in the County. They have before them a final report of the year before, and a status report on the year which is, by then, seven-eighths completed. They also have an estimate of participation for the coming year, based on 98 per cent of *fifth*-grade enrollments in March of the present year. This estimate for the current year, he said, was 15,265, and would have been pretty close except for the entrance of the two additional districts. Against that estimate, they then calculate the probable cost of staffing the program and teaching it. For the current year that esimate was $22 per child, and this amount was charged all parparticipating school districts on the basis of 98 per cent of their fifth-grade enrollments in March of the previous year — charged whether the child comes to camp or not. (In predicting actual attendance, they usually calculate about 94 per cent of the 98 per cent.) If a district with less than 200 sixth graders comes into the program, it can pay for the campers who actually use the service, he said, but at a higher rate — $23.50 instead of $22 per child.

"This way," he said, "we come to a figure which San Diego should put in its budget for its financing, and which La Mesa-Spring Valley should put in its budget as a basis for entering into contracts with other school districts in the county. Remember," he added, "this is for *teaching* services. It is entirely separate from the cost of food, nursing services, and the like, which are a part of what is handled by the Camp Commission, and is paid for by the parents."

Someone asked whether they could safely tell parents that *their* cost for next year will be approximately the same as for last year. Pumala said he couldn't answer that until more information was in the hands of the Camp Commission. Hall said it was his snap judgment that the cost would be within a dollar of what it was last year.

Shortly after that, he called for other questions, and adjourned the meeting.

The session was fast-moving, expertly chaired, with educators playing their professional roles and concentrating on educational policy problems, and not feeling the need to make speeches or interfere in the administrative duties of their camp principal, in whom they obviously felt a great deal of confidence. I mentioned this to the chairman, Dr. Hall, after the meeting, and asked what was his general impression of what the teachers and school administrators thought of the outdoor education program now that they had seen it a while.

"Three or four years ago we had a series of evaluation meetings," he said. "Basically it was to involve the teachers and use their good professional judgment as to whether this week of outdoor education and camping was in fact contributing to their instructional program. If the teachers had judged it a waste of time, we might well have abandoned the whole activity. But most of them had found not only that it contributed very materially to the social studies unit in conservation, but also there were many related benefits to be gained from being in a different setting, and getting an opportunity to learn to know their children better than they would have if they had been back in the stereotyped classroom setting. We were taking stock as to whether we had something that should be continued, or abandoned, or major modifications made in it. The result was very favorable."

"You're pretty confident, then, of where the program stands?"

"I think that as of now it is regarded almost universally throughout the county as a very special and desirable part of our public school program. Some years back I wouldn't have been quite as confident. As of now I am confident that the people in the city of San Diego want it to be kept as a part of the instructional program for our public schools, and most of the people in most of the districts outside the city feel the same way. I think it has come of age and become an accepted and approved program."

I was also able to catch Mr. Summers, from Chula Vista, as he was leaving the meeting, and asked him whether his district had made any evaluation of the outdoor educational program.

"No formal study," he said, "but the comments the principals pick up from the teachers often reflect their own evaluations, and our teachers have been very positive on this. We recognize that they sacrifice a little bit by having to go to camp. They are on a 24-hour day there, and occasionally they are at camp on a vacation day. Our district has made provision for this. In spite of this, though, our teachers think it is a wonderful experience. I can recall no very serious or at all derogatory remarks or unfavorable evaluations from teachers concerning the program. Occasionally they will disagree with how things are done up there at camp. This is fine. We feed this information back to the camp through the Advisory Committee."

I asked him how his campership program was going. He pointed out that his district had many minority group families.

"Nearly every PTA in the district donates one or more camperships every year, though," he said. "Generally we'll get one, two, three, possibly more camperships from certain service clubs. I think we have overcome that problem. There has recently been no youngster, I believe, kept back because he didn't have money to go. The same thing holds for the clothing and equipment they need. Sometimes they don't have shoes that are proper for camp. The camp carries a stock of galoshes for wet weather."

"Even after this, are there some of your children who don't go to camp?"

"I would guess we have about 90 per cent participation," he said. "Those who don't go, make that decision for personal or family reasons — sometimes religious, or the need of special medical care, or simply because the parents don't want their child to leave home for five days. I've even seen a few parents who wouldn't let their child go because this child had the responsibility of caring for a younger sister or brother at home. But it's not a financial reason. We bend over backwards to eliminate the good excuses for children not going. We believe in what the experience will do for them."

I called on Glenn Murdock, a soft-spoken man with graying sandy hair, who is Superintendent of the La Mesa-Spring Valley School District that shares with the San Diego City Schools the task of employing the camp teachers. He told me how the joint employment plan worked. When the Education Advisory Committee decides how many teaching positions are to be filled, and the total cost of instruction is computed, then La Mesa-Spring Valley enters into contracts with the other participating County school districts to cover their share of the cost of instruction. The contribution of each district is in proportion to its sixth-grade enrollment. The actual hiring La Mesa-Spring Valley has to do is about comparable to filling the entire staff of one of its own elementary schools — 15 to 20 teachers.

We find that teachers are not necessarily effective in both the outdoor and the classroom situation," he said. "A teacher who is good in the classroom is usually good in the camps, too. But sometimes it doesn't work in reverse. Sometimes a teacher who likes outdoor education and is skillful at it, does not like the restrictions of the classroom."

I asked what had been La Mesa-Spring Valley's own experience with its pupils in the outdoor education program. "We have been in it from the time it started," he said. "We consider it one of our finest programs because of its discovery approach to learning and its emphasis on science and conservation. Students look forward to their experience in camp for months or even years. When they return, their excitement and enthusiasm over and over again confirms our belief in the value of the experience for them."

I went also to see Dr. Cecil Hardesty who is County Superintendent of Schools. (Editor's Note: since the author wrote the foregoing, Dr. Hardesty has moved to Jacksonville, Florida, where he is Superintendent of the Duval County Schools.) He explained to me that in California the County Superintendent of Schools is a county official, standing between the school districts, and between school districts and other county officials. Thus each county school district will have its own superintendent and school board. But the County Superintendent is the only school official who, on certain occasions, has to speak for all the districts. I asked him what the school camping program meant to children from rural homes, who are more accustomed than city children to the outdoors.

"I think the youngsters who come from rural homes and small school districts are just as enthusiastic about it as youngsters from the city," he said firmly. "You get to take your sleeping bag and gear, and go up and sleep in a dormitory, and have the dining room experiences, and with the right kind of weather an outdoor campfire or an indoor deal with the fireplace at night. It's a big experience for these youngsters. I would venture that the youngsters from San Diego actually have learned more from the trip than youngsters, let's say, who live in a village or on a farm, but it doesn't mean that these other kids don't have an experience that's exciting and thrilling."

I asked him about problems in making the program go.

"Cooperation hasn't really been a problem," he said. "Financial problems have recurred. At times there has been reluctance, on the part of the City Council in particular, to go ahead and put money into the program. They are concerned with the issue that they pay a city tax to support it and city residents also pay the county tax. That has sometimes been a trouble. Then there has sometimes been a push to increase student fees and thus get more of the cost directly from the participating families. I resist this every time it comes up. We can make a case for charging the youngster enough for his board and room, but I don't think we can make a case for anything beyond that. So this has been a problem all through the years — trying to balance the budget.

"I'll tell you this," he said. "When there have been any reports, arising out of the budget problem, that the San Diego Unified School District might be forced to cut out the camping program from its budget, then the other county districts have quietly behind the scenes taken a position that if San Diego pulls out they'll still go ahead on some basis. We're not going to let this thing go down the drain."

I judged that to be a pretty general feeling.

# XIV
## A VISIT WITH THE CAMP COMMISSION

AT 8 A.M. ON THE FOLLOWING WEDNESDAY I was in the San Diego
County Supervisors chambers for the meeting of the Camp Commission.

*"Eight* o'clock?" I had asked Ed Pumala when he told me about
the meeting. He laughed and explained, "I catch these busy men
before they get busy."

Coffee and doughnuts were rewards for coming at this hour,
and over them I got acquainted with the members of the Commission. Dr. Hall was there representing the City Superintendent of
Schools, and a man from the County Superintendent's office represented Dr. Hardesty. The President of the Ninth District P.T.A.
was present. She explained to me that this organization was a
county council, representing all the 319 P.T.A. units, and the
110,000 members in San Diego County. I mentioned that I understood the P.T.A. had remodeled the staff lounge at Camp Palomar,
which I thought was now very attractive. She said this was cor-
rect; the lounge had been in "sad shape," and they had taken over
the task of making it livable. "All sorts of different things that no
one else does, we pick up," she explained. One of the things she
will be sorriest about when she retires from her two-year term in
the Presidency of the Ninth District, she said, is that then she will
be off the Camp Commission. The current President always serves
on the Commission. "You can't really understand the scope of the
program without working with it," she said. "You know that your
own sixth grader went to camp, and had a wonderful experience,
but you don't realize the effect it has on all the other children. I
just can't think of any other program, anywhere, that gives every
child something."

Edwin Pumala and Denver Fox were there. A man from Pumala's staff was serving as secretary of the meeting. Mr. Walsh, from
the City Council, was not able to be present because of illness, but
a man from the City Planning Office was sitting in. And just after
8:00, De Graff Austin, the chairman, arrived.

Austin is one of the founding fathers of the camping and outdoor education program. On the Commission he represents the
Board of County Supervisors, of which he is an elected member,
but he came into the program before there was a Commission or
a school camp, even before Pumala was hired, and the outdoor
education program has been a continuing chapter in his long civic

career. Seeing him in a group you might think he looks grand-fatherly (he is a grandfather, several times over). Talking to him you realize that he exudes an atmosphere of kindness and friend-liness, he is a skilled raconteur, a relaxed man, a comfortable man to be with, and yet underneath the relaxation there is a great drive that keeps coming to the surface whenever a problem arises. Along with the benevolence, he communicates a sense of "let's get along with it . . . I'll do this . . . you do this . . . we'll get John to do this . . ." And before long, a problem solution begins to appear.

Talking to him before the meeting, I mentioned that I was try-ing to understand the organization and operation of the program. "It's very loosely organized," he said with a smile. "One of my neighbors, a priest in the Catholic Church, said, 'It's typical of you: It's organized like the Congregational Church,' of which I am a member. Each congregation determines for itself what it is going to do. It's loose, but it's a picture of cooperative effort — two school agencies, the lay people of the communities, the city government, the county government, the state for a landlord. And we just make them work together, and dare anybody to get out! Fiscal matters have come up for scrutiny several times, though, and we have de-veloped a pretty tight system of controls for handling all our fiscal affairs."

He sat down in his seat, and moved smoothly into the meeting. The room where we met was considerably different from the set-ting of the Advisory Committee meeting. The Supervisors' cham-bers were designed for public meetings and hearings. Walls were panelled in dark wood. A massive bench for the Supervisors faced tables for witnesses and officials, and behind them tiered rows of seats for spectators. For this meeting the room was made to seem somewhat less formal by assembling the Commission members at a large square table pushed up against the bench.

There were no spectators except two reporters and me.

Austin asked for a report on the progress of work on Camp David-son. Pumala said it was coming along well. The two new districts have done a good job in preparing. Their schedule will be out to-day or tomorrow. He noted that they are providing some kitchen equipment which is lacking at Camp Davidson. "But I particularly want to commend Denver for his scrounging," he said. "I think he is one of the best scroungers we have. He has not only gotten stoves and deep freezes for the new camp, but also other materials, and figured out a way to have tables made out of some of the extra tables we have at Palomar. So it appears that the physical plant at Camp Davidson will be ready providing we get all the things we think we're going to get."

One thing lacking, he said, is a bus. He spoke of various possibilities, none of them very good. Austin came alert at the problem. "Concerning your need for a bus," he said, "you might start running it down through our Commissioner." (He mentioned the name.) "The City," he said, "has just acquired for its transit system a hundred new buses, and hasn't disposed of the old ones. We might for a very nominal sum charter one of those — maybe five dollars a month for the school year. You get after Jack; I'll talk to the president and manager. It might be they could just put one out there for the good of the cause. Would you do that, Ed?"

He passed on to the next matter. A master plan for development of the state parks will be presented before the end of the present legislative session, he said. So far, negotiations on plans for the school camps have gone smoothly. "Every time we have discussed any particular problem with them," he said, "our plans have fallen right in line with what he expects to do. We've been cooperating, revamping the building proposals to meet their suggestions. I have one of the most cordial letters acknowledging the splendid cooperation they have had from Mr. Pumala and Mr. Gardner and the County generally, and willing to go all out in our behalf. This includes a willingness to put in a swimming pool at Cuyamaca." They talked these matters over, and Austin advised saving a place in the plans for the pool, but holding back until the master plan itself was approved before seeking the pool.

He asked for a report on the Education Advisory Committee, and Dr. Hall gave an admirably succinct account of what had happened the previous week. Denver Fox then spoke about the effect on the construction schedule on the outdoor education and the summer programs in the camps. He pointed out that the presence of construction workers with all their equipment will make a great difference in what kind of program can go on there.

Hall picked up the topic, and said that the time of completion was indeed a matter of real urgency. "If the major construction can be completed before the first of November," he said, "we can schedule all the children, including the two additional districts, into three camps with their enlarged facilities. Conversely, we are of the opinion that if the construction cannot be completed before the first of November, we are probably in need of facing up to the rental or leasing of a fourth camp, with all the inefficiencies of unit costs that go into that operation."

Pumala said this is indeed a real problem, because in the last week the probable schedule of construction had been extended. The report now is, he said, that they may not be able to get the bids out until the middle of June, whereas they had hoped to get started on the project by the first of May at the latest. So these worries are well founded.

This turned out to be the main discussion of the meeting. Austin reviewed the situation. The writing of the joint powers agreement which would make possible the sale of bonds was going slowly, he said; it was temporarily bogged down on the detail of language outlining the responsibility of the camp commission to pick up rubbish. He told a Frank Capra story to relieve some of the tension, and then began to examine the possibility of hurrying the process along. "It's the chairman's function as straw boss to pick up the ends and see that arrangements get hurried along," he said. "If we work everything right and drive hard enough to have it, we are going to have a great interest on the part of the associated general contractors to get in and see that the proper person gets this bid, and give him every bit of cooperation." He reported some conversations he had been having with contractors and suppliers.

"So I think the thing for us to do," he concluded the discussion, "is to drive, drive, drive, on the actual construction work of the buildings. It wouldn't surprise me if by the time school opens in the fall we could have an appreciable part of the construction accomplished."

I was not so hopeful, but found myself being carried along by the chairman's energy and determination.

Several appointments to the food service staffs of the camps were approved, and also a long list of permits for groups and organizations to reserve the camps on weekends or in the summer. It was interesting to note the variety of users of the camps during the times when the camp schools were not operating. A group from the College Park Presbyterian Church were going to Camp Palomar for a weekend in February. The Forward H Square Dance Group were going to be at Cuyamaca for a weekend in March. The Junior R.O.T.C. of the San Diego School District were camping at Cuyamaca a weekend in April. The next weekend, the San Diego Council of Camp Fire Girls were to be there. The National Science Foundation was sponsoring a week-end camp at Palomar in May. The "Y" Indian Guides of the Downtown Y.M.C.A., Grossmont High School, Temple Beth Israel, the American Camping Association, the American Lutheran Church Men, were also among the week-end campers whose reservations were approved by the Commission. Some summer reservations also were on the list. Among these were the Camp Fire Girls of Oceanside, the San Diego Association for Retarded Children, the Christian Family Group, and the Jewish Community Center. These were going to Cuyamaca or Palomar for a week each.

A report on cost of meals at the camps was accepted, and then they turned to the one major item remaining — the election of a new chairman for the Commission. To no one's surprise, De Graff Austin was nominated and elected to succeed himself. Hall referred to him as "a politician in the most admirable sense — a ramrod, expediter, an encourager, of bringing public forces to bear on very worthwhile achievements."

"This is the quickest and most concise campaign I have ever waged," Austin said. "With unbecoming modesty, I accept. We are right in the middle of something, and I would like to conclude it, and make my project this year as a supervisor to see that we at long last have our youngsters off the hills in safe housing."

He reminisced a little while about the program.

"A time for leisure and rest."

"We have had an inspiring program for a long while," he said, "and to think of how it came to be! This was before we even thought of a Commission. A group of us, with the blessing and participation of Dr. Carroll, the Superintendent of Schools, and with Chester Van Dusen, of the Boys Club, volunteering his vacation, borrowed the old County road camp that had been abandoned. It was at the upper end of the grade in the Laguna Mountains. We took 29 boys, mixed as to ethnic origin, out to that old place for a month's camping. None of them had even gone to camp, but 18 of them had been in trouble with the law during the preceding year. And we enlisted the City fire department. They were on the two-platoon system, as they are now — 24 hours on and 24 hours off — and we took the matter to their Association, and they filled in and provided the leadership. Van Dusen went out and spent all his time there, and my responsibility was to circulate among the wholesale houses in the lower end of town, particularly the produce houses, to pick up for free at the end of the sales period each morning the food for the outfit. We put together a program that some of the old-time firemen still laugh about — how they were hi-jacked into the assignment, and how beautifully they performed. And do you know that we checked through the following year, and not a one of those boys who had been in trouble with the law before, got into trouble again!

"The second summer we took 42 boys to camp, and they followed about the same pattern. The firemen made it a point to take some little groups here, there, everywhere — trips along the coast of Lower California, for instance, where it was easier to get to, and they could partly live off the land as they went along. And out of this grew the notion that something must be done in this area. So Will Crawford who was then the City Superintendent of Schools, and John Carroll, the County Superintendent of Schools, and I — I was on the City Council then — we were delegated to get down and organize a commission. And so the discussion led to this kind of commission where we could involve more and more people, and make it very awkward for them to withdraw, and easy for them to expand. And out of those first summer camp periods came the leasing of Cuyamaca, and the idea that a school camp would be something pretty splendid. So here we are. I can't think of a more generous contribution than the school system has made in pioneering this and getting it done, bearing in mind that it's a costly venture, and I've seen supervisors and councilmen scratch their heads and squirm about this measly little administration budget. But we've had more than 250,000 children go through these camps now, and have been in business long enough to have had two of the present City Councilmen as boys — sixth graders— in the camps, and many of our prominent businessmen have been to camp and know what the experience means. I hope there can never be a withdrawal now from the notion that any individual who fails to have even this brief period of outdoor education is a neglected person!"

After a few routine questions, the meeting was adjourned.

"Sorry Jack Walsh wasn't here," the chairman said to me afterward. "Go see him. Ask him how the Council feels about it."

So I did, when Mr. Walsh got back to his office. He turned out to be a big, genial man, who had an enlarged picture of his family covering one whole panel of the wall. It was one of the kinds of pictures you could use if there were any need to start another migration to California: handsome, tanned, athletic parents, and a very large number of children, tanned, happy, and healthy looking. "One more since then," he said. "Seven now."

I asked him the question De Graff Austin had suggested: what did the City Council think of the program.

"I went to the Camp Commission," he said, "with a sort of prenotion that it was not long for the world. My predecessor in office in the district had served on the Commission also, and he had made presentations to the Council saying at the extension of the lease, or maybe even before that, maybe the City should be getting out. One of the main objections was that we, as citizens of San Diego, pay city taxes and county taxes. Therefore, we are paying double for our contribution to the camps.

"I went into it, and it wasn't very long after being involved with the program, and possibly because I had five children then and seven now, that I became more interested in the needs for camping and what it can do. So I got involved with the Commission activities, did a little bit of research, and rather than recommending to the Council the elimination of our City participation, I made a prolonged presentation over a number of conferences on why we should be in it.

"And with the modification of our participation based on a formula that would carry our participation both as County and as City taxpayers, we convinced the Council to go ahead and get involved. The further we went into it, we saw the need for capital improvements. The buildings up there were something of a disgrace. More important, they were a safety hazard. So out of that came calling of a conference, and the idea of allocating a million five over a number of years to put in the needed capital improvements."

"How much money does the City put in?" I asked him.

"Varying amounts," he said. "Initially we put in more. We have come to a recognized policy that we ask the Commission to make the fees at least cover the operating expenses. And so City participation has been on a fluctuating basis, because we have gone to just the capital improvements, and it may some years be 19 thousand and some years over 100 thousand. Now we are committing ourselves over a period of time, in cooperation with the County, for about a million and a half dollars. And this would be pretty much our commitment for, say, the next 15 years."

I asked him what kind of feedback he got on the program from his constituents.

"The feedback is minimal," he said. "It's just like good government. When you don't hear people complaining, everything is going fine. In this program if you need any political support, or testimony to the need of the program or its benefit, all you have to do is to make one mention in the press that there is some concern, and there is a flood of letters. The people who have benefited from the program come out of hiding, so to speak."

I asked him what advice he would have for another city contemplating a program of outdoor education like San Diego's.

"My advice would be, look at the mistakes we made, and don't make the same ones," he said. "Review the history of what we have done and what other camps have done. We've had a lot of problems over 20 years, but we've been able to iron them out, and anybody who has an idea of such a program has a good model. As a real clincher, before you make any sort of proposal, come out and spend three or four days at one of the campsites. Walk around as a sort of shadow, trail some of the kids, see the expressions, find out what they are doing, and see what you think. If that doesn't convince an individual of the merit of these camps, then they shouldn't go ahead with the program.

"Then you've got to have some individuals that see beyond what's right immediately in front of them. I think it's necessary that you have inspired leadership, not just ordinary leadership, because in a program like this you've got to have people that get worked up about it. If they're good leaders but can't get themselves worked up about it, they should step aside. But if you've got that kind of leadership, then I think the limits that will be placed upon the program are very small, because the excitement will make you find ways to get around the problems."

He was going to play tennis at lunch time. I was going to eat a San Diego fish. We went toward our respective goals.

# XV
# WHAT CHILDREN RETAIN FROM THE EXPERIENCE

I HAD TWO MORE STOPS TO MAKE. One building was almost in sight of the bay, the other on the flat land to the east. One was behind a row of palms, the other behind an enormous asphalt playground. But I recognized them as members of the same genus and species — California elementary schools, sleek and single-story, rows of windows open to the balmy air, green chalkboards carefully shaded from the sun, and looking always as though built exactly five years ago. These were the schools that had sent their sixth grades to Cuyamaca while I was there.

I knew I was on a forlorn quest. Any lasting changes that the camps had made in the children would be too subtle or too long-range to be detected by a single visit. One could hardly expect any fundamental change anyway; after all, the camping experience was only five days out of 12 or 13 years during which the influences of the family, the community, the church, the school, and the peer group had been imprinted on the children. Yet I wanted to fill in, as well as I could, the unfinished parts of my picture: What did these children look like outside camp? And what happened after the camping experience?

In each school soon I began to see children I knew — by sight if not by name. Here was Maria, prettier than ever with her long dark hair and olive skin set off by a green and gold school dress. Here was Yankees, in a pink sport shirt rather than his baseball jacket. Sally waved at me; she was wearing a white sweater rather than the blue one that took my eye at camp. The boy who played the guitar for Northwind was rushing to an orchestra practice. A blonde girl came up to ask what things were like at camp now; had there been any more rain or snow? She seemed to think I lived there. And there was Dan, handsome and sullen as ever.

"Well, how did you like it?" I asked him.

"I really liked it," he said.

"What did you like best?"

"The hikes were best. And it was fun to make new friends, even fellows from La Mesa."

"Did you like the teachers up there?"

"Yes, I did. I liked them all, even Harry. And you know what *he* made me do. But I've stayed out of trouble. Tell everybody hello for me, will you?" he said.

The sixth-grade teachers looked visitor-like no longer. "How is it to come home?" I asked them. They said they missed the mountain air, but it was nice to get out of a sleeping bag and into one's own bed.

Had the children been much different, since camp? You can't expect miracles out of a single week, they said. The science classes had been better — they all agreed on this. One of the classes had even been planning a field trip. Conservation was real, now that the children had done some of it. They had brought back a lot of exhibits for the tables and the bulletin boards. Some of the classes had made reports of their experience, one to the PTA, another to an assembly. And they had written a lot of themes and letters about camp. Would I like to read some of the letters?

"What happens to pond life in the winter?"

Indeed, I would. There were even a few letters to me. But most of the letters were written to the camp teachers. The choices seemed to be spread over *all* the teachers. Some were addressed to a group of them — "Hi Roy, Ernie, Harry," or "Dear Dottie, Isabel, Jay, and Nurse Carol." But the whole sweep of counselors were apparently liked well enough to have letters addressed to them. One boy even asked Harry to hand his letter around to the other counselors, because he was afraid they might feel bad if they didn't hear from him. Mostly the boys wrote to the male teachers, the girls to the females, but not entirely. For example:

Dear Jennie:

You were my best counselor because you were very nice, and very pretty, and had a good personality and a very good figure.

I like Dick because he's a nice guy but he doesn't have a good figure.

Most of the reactions weren't that mature. This was more typical:

I think I shall always remember the hike I went on and saw three deer. I will remember the Monkey Bridge and the songs we sang. But most of all I will remember the camp itself no matter how you change it.

And this:

When I got there I wanted to come home a little, but later I changed my mine. I wish I could stay two weeks there.

Another:

If I had another chance to go to camp I would go. I especially liked conservation, but on the most part the camp was planned and very enjoyable.

I also found that washing dishes was quite fun, and so I enjoyed camp more than anything in my whole life.

Hikes, conservation, and the Monkey Bridge were mentioned perhaps oftener than anything else, but all the other activities

"All together, let's move it!"

"We learned about animals first-hand."

came in for praise also. Leafing through the papers, one read
things like these:

> Monday was a fun day when I arrived at camp. That is when I
> started to get used to the ways of life up there. We started to un-
> pack and then we went out and played.
> While I was up at camp we didn't see very many animals but a lot
> of small ones like the squirrel, woodrat, redtailed hawks, rabbit, and
> lots of tracks. Then on hikes I saw a lot of different kinds of trees like
> the manzanita, black oak, yellow pine, live oak, seedling trees, and
> lots of others.
> I'll tell the thing I enjoyed the most was the Monkey Bridge. It was
> not no ordinary bridge, it was made to be fun and boy is it! And on
> rainy days or when the sun was out we would go and fix it. And that
> was fun too.
>
> \* \* \* \* \*
>
> I think that the most interesting thing at camp was geology since
> it is a hobbie. It also helped me on my geology merit badge for scout-
> ing. Rock craft was very interesting to.
> I think everybody accomplished something at camp. The fact that
> we all did conservation at some time is one. Camp was the most fun
> and interesting thing I ever did while in school.
>
> \* \* \* \* \*
>
> I enjoyed camp and if I had another chance to go I would go. But
> I enjoyed conservation the most of all. Because you learned the true
> meaning of conservation. Which is to protect, presurve, and use wise-
> ly our natural resources. Also when you got there you didn't start
> chopping down a tree. First you learned the names of the tools, how
> to use them and how to carry them. Then after lunch you had a quick
> review of your tools and went to work.

* * * * *

What I didn't like so much at camp was conservation. The only thing I didn't like about it was chopping down the trees and working all day. But in a way I did like it because it taught me more about the beetles and termites and how we can prevent the fires in the forest.

* * * * *

I thought I learned more than I would at school any day, because out of doors you can see so much but in school you get bored reading out of books.

I think I learned most about the Dieguenos, because I took Indian Lore and Indian crafts. I like all the counselors very much!

"Do si do your partner!"

There were occasional negative notes:

> On thing I didn't like were the heaters, they sounded like tidle waves and you couldn't get to sleep.

* * * * *

> At night it was very hard to get to sleep because of the animal sounds and the wind brushing through the trees. At that time I was able to think freely. Usually I was thinking of the comfortable bed at home.

* * * * *

> The part that I didn't like was that I thought you could just wander around, but you couldn't. You had to go by classes. But they made sure you learned what the camp offered. And the part I liked was the counselors and the meals.

There was no doubt they approved of the food. Perhaps one out of every four papers mentioned it, but not always so vividly as this:

> The chop suey the cooks cook was really good. One girl that sat by me ate about 5 or 6 helpings of it. I wouldn't blame her. The banana pudding was good too. And one time on hikes the same girl fell in the water.
>
> I really had a good time down there.

There were frequent mentions of making new friends.

It's been a few weeks since I left camp and last saw you. A few things I have come to realize about camp are now coming into use. I learned to make friends easily with your help. Camp has helped me make friends with new and different people.

Some of them wrestled with trying to say what had happened to them, in big terms like "personality" and "responsibility." Some said they had gained in self-control because "I learned not to want to kill somebody when he broke my guitar string," or "I learned not to get mad when someone shoved me." Some mentioned that they found it more fun than they had expected, to do something for someone — for example:

I found it was fun to clean up a bed for somebody when he had to stay and do dishes and didn't get back for cleanup.

They spoke of cabin loyalty, too, like this boy:

Southwind may have lost points on cleanup but it was still a good cabin.
Thank you. I told everyone how much fun I had last week. That was my first time of being away.

And this was not an uncommon sentiment:

Hi, how are you? It must be fun to be at camp all year long. I would like to be a counselor when I grow up.

The classroom teachers also spoke in praise of the camp teachers. One San Diego teacher summed it up in his evaluation by saying that teachers at camp treated the children with "firmness, respect and human kindness," and this made a great difference in the quality of the camp experience.

At La Mesa the participating classes conducted their own opinion poll. The children answered without signing their names. Most of the results were simply favorable comments, and about as overwhelming as attitude surveys ever get. For example:

I told my younger brothers and sisters (or friends) that they should go to school camp when they are in the 6th grade.
AGREE 57        UNDECIDED 2        DISAGREE 4

Some of the questions, however, pointed at sources of less than complete satisfaction:

I had enough free time to do as I pleased.
AGREE 24        UNDECIDED 9        DISAGREE 31

A few of the questions tried to tap some of the changes that camp had helped bring about:

Guarding our forests against fires means more to me now that I have lived in the forest.
AGREE 53        UNDECIDED 4        DISAGREE 4

Since I went to camp, I felt that I am getting along better with the boys and girls in my class.
AGREE 34        UNDECIDED 18        DISAGREE 11

I feel differently about my teacher after going to class with him.
AGREE 34        UNDECIDED 17        DISAGREE 12

I asked the classroom teachers whether camp really *had* made a difference in their relationship to the children. They said it had. They knew the pupils better and more personally, and had a common experience to talk about. One of the teachers repeated what she had told me at camp, that she would give anything if she could have the camping time early in the fall, so as to build on that experience during the rest of the school year.

Did they see evidence of changes in behavior or values as a result of camp? Here they were less certain. "One boy's mother told me he doesn't put his elbows on the table any more," a teacher reported with a laugh. "Chalk up one score for the dining room!" A San Diego teacher summed up what seemed to be the general feeling: You can't expect a fundamental change in a week. If a boy has been running with a bad gang, he sinks back into that pattern when he comes back from camp. If a child has been made insecure or hostile in a hostile or broken home, camp will not change that. But in general, such changes as you can feel are good. Some of the children seem to be nicer, friendlier kids. Some of them seem to try to get along better. They have more things to be interested in. They seem especially to have more interest in the outdoors and in natural things.

"Actually, then, you saw more changes in camp than you see here," I said. They said they did. In camp the surrounding environment had been changed, and so behavior could be more easily changed; back home, the old environment enforces its own behavior.

"But look," said one of the teachers. "Remember it's just a *week* in camp. How much change do you see in a week in the classroom? Compared to that, the change you see, or at least the potential for change, in a week at camp is enormous. It's a change. It's a break. It's a new and different experience. It's terribly important to some of them."

I asked about some of the students I knew. It was true, they said, that Dan and some of the other boys hadn't gotten into any more trouble, although they were crossing their fingers on that matter. Yes, Money-back and one or two of the boys seemed to be a little less loud now. George? "How is little George?" I asked. "Has his father come back from Vietnam yet?"

They looked at me oddly.

"Didn't you know?" George's teacher said. "His daddy was killed in Vietnam about six months ago. He was on that base the VC bombarded. Camp was good for George. He was so lonely before, and seems a little less lost now."

\*　　\*　　\*　　\*　　\*

That night, at a motel in San Diego Bay, with grey ships of the fleet anchored to one side of the island and yachts tied up, gunwale to gunwale, on the other, I tried to put together what I had seen and heard.

I had seen boys and girls going through an important experience at the school camps — of that I had no doubt. As the teachers pointed out, it was only one week out of 12 or 13 years. But it was a week that made nature real to asphalt-dwellers. It was a week that opened to them a way of learning, and offered them a chance to gain insights into themselves and into the problems of living with other people. If the classrooms make wise use of that experience, then school will never again be quite the same for these children. And the children themselves will never be quite the same, even though one week will not cancel out influences or qualities that are much older and deeper.

I came away from the camps with a considerable admiration for the teachers and the teaching. Rethinking merely deepened this impression. Twelve- and thirteen-year olds are highly imitative; exposing them to the strength, kindness, and learning orientation of these attractive teachers, and to their belief in democratic living, may well be one of the most significant parts of the school camp experience. And as for the problem-solving, "discovery" teaching — well, that is an experience I covet for my own children.

Furthermore, exposing the children to a meaningful conservation experience, and to the contrast between natural beauty and wastage, may ultimately have a profound effect on the policy San Diego adopts toward the preservation of its natural heritage as it grows toward megalopolis.

I had little remaining doubt as to what San Diego felt about the outdoor education program. The parents, the school and community leaders, were convinced. They were behind it. It occurred to me that it was significant that I was not seeing a new program, but rather a program more than 20 years old. If it could still arouse, after 20 years, the kind of enthusiasm and dedication I had observed, then it must have certain deep and lasting qualities.

But on the basis of what I had seen and heard, what advice would I give another city or county or school district that thought of starting a program of outdoor education? What is the essence of the San Diego experience that is worth passing on to another potential user?

I recalled something that Denver Fox had said to me as we rode back to Camp Marston from the desert. He said that when a community is starting a program like this, the first requirement is that someone in the community or the district has to become *convinced* — convinced both that this kind of program has value, and convinced sufficiently so that he can convince several other sets of people. I think that is what Councilman Walsh, too, meant when he said that a program like this needs people "who get worked up about it."

What an extraordinary number of dedicated people have had a part in the history of outdoor education in San Diego City and County! De Graff Austin told the Camp Commission, in his little speech of acceptance, how the program came into being through the dedication of a few public-spirited citizens. But this spirit prevailed not only in the early days. One cannot spend a day in one of the camps without realizing that the present teaching staffs also display a high order of dedication. After 20 years.

Of course, the leaders of the program have passed that spirit on. San Diego has been fortunate in having, for so many years, skilled and dedicated professionals like Edwin Pumala and Denver Fox. I have no way of knowing this, but assume that Pumala, with the powerful support of top leadership, has been the chief instrument of broad community involvement in the program; and Fox, with the powerful support of school leadership and the Commission, has been the chief architect of the teaching and learning opportunities that exist in the camp schools. I suppose that if I could wish one blessing for a community starting such a program anew I would wish that they might have two leaders like Pumala and Fox — and the support those two have had.

One unusual feature of the San Diego experience, however, has been the diffusion of significant leadership through many segments of the community. When Austin was describing the first years of the program, he paid appropriate tribute to the leadership exerted by the City Superintendent of Schools, the County Superintendent, himself, and others, even before it was possible to bring Pumala and later Fox into the picture. As Walsh said, throughout the history of the program there always seemed to be leaders who would emerge when the program needed them. And strong leadership is still being exerted today by school administrators, elective officials, and representatives of civic organizations.

At some point or other, of course, breadth of leadership merges with community support and cooperation, and San Diego obviously has had these. By some means or other, divisive tendencies and self-serving policies have been overcome — perhaps, as Dr. Dailard said, by "men of good will." In a sense, the very breadth and extent of cooperation, and the sharing of responsibility, may have made the job harder: A program where the funding and responsibilities are divided among many organizations and official bodies is likely to be harder to administer than one where there is a simple line of authority and support. On the other hand, the diffusion of responsibility and support has made the San Diego program stronger than any of its components, and built political and financial stability. I recalled what the County Superintendent told me: that at one time when it was feared that San Diego might have to pull out of the program for financial reasons, the county schools had quietly determined that if this happened they would go it alone by some means; they would not let the program go down the drain. A number of people recalled that any time the program was threatened, a great wave of support arose from the community.

So the San Diego program has had the benefit of dedicated, skillful leadership, and very wide community participation and support. These are blessings we could wish for any new program. But suppose one seeks more specific advice about starting such a program: What can one learn from the San Diego experience?

I have had many talks on this question, in San Diego, and from my notes I could almost put together dialogue — one that never happened, of course, but might have.

*Denver Fox:* Someone must become convinced.

*Edwin Pumala:* And they must settle on a clear set of objectives. What does the community want out of a program? For instance, school camping is a kind of misnomer; it sounds like something in school time that could just as well be done without wasting school time. Actually, San Diego has established school camps so that it could have camp *schools*. Its program transplants school, not just pupils, to the mountains for a week. The community understands this, but we had to understand it before we could take it to the community.

*George Hall:* When you are making the first plans is a good time to find out what other school districts and committees have done with outdoor education.

*Denver Fox:* If it is decided by the key people that this is something the community or the district needs and is willing to pay for, the first thing they had better do is to get good leadership — right from the beginning, so that the planning is sound. They should bring in someone who has vision, experience in outdoor living, an idea of the educational potential of such activity. Someone who can guide the development and begin to recommend people to form a nucleus of a staff.

*Jack Walsh:* You've got to have inspired leadership.

*Edwin Pumala:* But you must broaden the leadership and the

involvement as soon as possible. Let us say that the nuclear group has arrived at a clear idea of objectives, and has decided that it is going to be a school program. Once you have obtained the approval of the Board of Education, the Superintendent, then directly the principals and the curriculum people should be involved, and other people and organizations like the Parent-Teacher Association. The leaders of the community must be informed and involved, because they will be the ones who will interpret the program to the community. The broader base of understanding you have, the easier your job is going to be. This takes time. But take time to let every member of the City Council, the Mayor, the Board of Supervisors, the business and civic leaders including the Chamber of Commerce, the service clubs, the Taxpayers Association — let them know in detail what is being planned, and if possible encourage them to enter into the planning and prepraation. Take the mass media into your confidence, and try to get them to recognize that this is something vital to the community. Give all these people full recognition for what they do in the program. And then make sure that the story is told to the community, by the media, by P.T.A. meetings, by teachers' meetings, by service clubs, and every means at your disposal.

*De Graff Austin:* Make them work together and dare them to get out!

*Ralph Dailard:* Be sure of your curricular tie-in with the schools when you plan the content of the outdoor education.

*Denver Fox:* My advice would be to start modestly. Make sure the experience is going to be successful, because if it isn't, it is going to retard outdoor education in that community for a long time. It is possible to start with no more than a few schools — those that are truly interested. It is possible even to start without residential facilities. If you start with a few interested schools, you are likely to have an excellent experience, and other schools will want to come in; whereas, if you make it district-wide at once, it might bring in enough people who don't want to go in, to sink the ship. Above all, try to have a program of high quality — no matter how big or how small — from the first.

*Tom Brown:* When someone comes to me about starting a program, usually the first question I ask is, What kind of staffing are you going to have? These people are on the firing line. They should be topnotch people. Ultimately, the quality of the program depends on them. If our program had not been a quality program, I'm convinced it would have gone down the drain, long ago.

*Edwin Pumala:* There's no cookbook for this sort of thing.

There's no recipe that can be used in all areas.

*Denver Fox:* You've got to find the combination that best fits your situation.

*Edwin Pumala:* One thing that can be learned from the San Diego experience is that there is a great positive gain in using the facilities and capabilities as widely as possible. Here we have 15,000 to 17,000 sixth graders using the camps on school days, but in addition we have nearly 5,000 people using the camps on weekends in the winter, and nearly 3,000 more in summer camp. This has been a powerful factor in broadening service to the community and community interest and involvement in the program.

That was the kind of advice I was remembering that night as I watched the moon descend toward San Diego bay. If I might contribute to the dialogue, it would be to wish that anyone contemplating a program of outdoor education could have the experience I had just had, of spending a little while in the San Diego school camps — or, let us say, camp schools. There is a rich mine of experience in the 20 years of the San Diego program. There is history. There are materials and guides and teachers' handbooks. There are experienced people to talk to. There is the recollection of many problems and how they were solved. But most important, there is the ongoing program in the camps. And this is the test of the effort and the organization: What happens to the children in five days of outdoor education and cabin living? I have tried to recapture this extraordinary experience as best I can, in this book, but I wish that readers might have the pleasure of seeing it for themselves.

# A Few Suggestions for Further Reading and Looking about the Program Described in This Book

*Outdoor Education: A Guide to the Instructional Program at the Sixth-Grade School Camps.* Prepared by Denver C. Fox, at the request of the Outdoor Education Advisory Committee. San Diego, California: San Diego City Schools, revised 1966.

*Teachers' Guide to Outdoor Education, Grade VI.* Prepared by Denver C. Fox, at the request of the Joint Outdoor Education Advisory Committee for 1966-67. San Diego, California: San Diego City Schools, revised 1966.

*Outdoor Education.* Filmstrip with taped narration. San Diego, California: San Diego City Schools, 1965.

*Pictures by* Department of County Schools, San Diego
Department of City Schools, San Diego
Denver C. Fox, Principal of the Camps, San Diego
Charles Aqua Viva, San Diego